Understanding American Poetry

Koichi Fujino
C. S. Pugh
Matt Theado
Michiko Takahashi

EIHŌSHA

音声ファイルのダウンロード方法

英宝社ホームページ（http://www.eihosha.co.jp/）の
「テキスト音声ダウンロード」バナーをクリックすると、
音声ファイルダウンロードページにアクセスできます。

Introduction

Who cares about poetry these days?

Perhaps many people today would say they do not ever read or listen to poetry, so it doesn't really mean anything to them. Poetry is just something from long ago, they say, or maybe just something they study occasionally in a literature class. But is that really the complete truth? It might be said that almost everyone listens to poetry every day, and feels that it is deeply important.

Think about it. When you go to a university entrance ceremony, one of the first things that happens is the playing and singing of the school song. A young couple has their first baby, and they take the newborn child to the shrine, where a priest performs a ceremony that includes …. Right, poetry. A grandparent dies, or a company begins building a new building, and there will be some poetry to make the occasion special and meaningful.

And that is not all. On a cold autumn night maybe you will hear someone selling sweet potatoes with a short poetic melody: "Yakiimo, yakiimoooo!" Or maybe the song is on TV selling something quite different and modern. And what about that sports team practicing? They run together singing a poem as simple as can be, "Ichi ni, ichi ni," but those simple words mean much more, don't they? "We are a team and we know how to work hard together in order to win our next game."

The list could go on, but you get the idea. Words are put together with special sounds and rhythms, in order to create and communicate a deep feeling of significance. That's what poetry is, and it is everywhere, once we begin to look for it. This textbook is meant to help you find poems and understand them better, and in particular it looks closely at some poems from one nation, the United States.

Probably all people who have ever lived, even if they do not realize it, have shared poetry as a part of their lives. It is part of what makes us human. Maybe the examples in this book will help you discover something about what Americans think and feel is important, but these poems may also have much to tell you about yourself and your own country's poetic world. Enjoy!

はしがき

　この教科書はアメリカ詩の理解を通してアメリカ文化を学ぶことを目的につくられました。同時に、詩を理解するための幾つかの設問に答えたのち、詩の内容についての考察を短い英文で書く訓練を通じて、物事を多角的・多面的に考える能力、いわゆるクリティカル・シンキングの力を身につけられるようにしています。どうぞ詩の内容を楽しみながら、世界を様々な視点から見る力を身につけてください。

　アメリカの詩をあまりよく知らなくても、まずは、この教科書に収められた詩を幾つか読んでみてください。かならず自分なりに理解できる詩に出会うことができると思います。また、詩は、それぞれが小さいながらも独自の世界をもった文学作品です。その内容をいくつかの視点から検討してみることは、クリティカル・シンキングの実践的な訓練になるでしょう。

　このテキストは次のような構成になっています。

1) 詩の楽しみ方についての英文ガイド

　詩はあまり読んだことがない、あるいはアメリカ詩の楽しみ方がよくわからない、という人も多いと思います。この教科書では、アメリカ詩にどのように接して良いかわからない人へのヒントとして、詩の楽しみ方についての英文ガイドを、Introduction、および3章が終わるごとに Guide 1〜5 として配置しています。まず、この部分を読むことからアメリカ詩の世界に入ってゆくのもよいでしょう。

2) 単語力養成

　それぞれの単元の最初に、詩の理解に役立つ単語力を養成するための Word Power を設けています。選択肢は5つしかありませんから、クイズ感覚で同じ意味になりそうな語句を線で結んでみましょう。

3) 詩の内容理解

　Warm-up Activity では、単語を使った穴埋め、あるいは語の並べ替えをして、詩の内容の要約を完成させます。

4) 詩の内容についての考察

　Questions では、詩の内容についての問いに答えます。問いをヒントにして、自分なりにその詩が何を伝えたいかを「発見」したり、その詩で何と何が「対比」されているかを考えてみてください。ここでは、詩をより良く味わうと同時に、クリティカル・シンキングの実践を行います。自分の書く英文の冒頭にその「発見」や「対比」をはっきりと簡潔に書くことができるようになると、それをトピック・センテンスにして、英語のパラグラフを書き進めていくことができます。

　この教科書は、アメリカ詩を楽しむばかりでなく、その内容を通じてアメリカ文化を学び、さらに実践的な思考能力や英語による発信能力の訓練ができるようデザインされています。この教科書でアメリカ詩に親しみ、将来にわたって、英語で文章や詩を書くことを楽しんだり、あるいは英語による詩や文学作品を出版する人が現れてくれることを願っています。

　最後になりましたが、このテキストの作成にあたっては、西南学院大学の学内 GP の助成と九州アメリカ文学会の協力を賜り、また、英宝社の佐々木元氏より、多大なご理解とお力添えをいただきました。ここに心からの感謝を捧げたいと思います。

2018年秋

著 者 一 同

Contents

Lesson 1 American Lives and Loves ———— 7

Lesson 2 School Life in America ———— 14

Lesson 3 Mother ———— 21

Lesson 4 Love (1) ———— 28

Lesson 5 Love (2) ———— 36

Lesson 6 Suicide, Sickness, and Death ———— 43

Lesson 7 Nature ———— 50

Lesson 8 Losses in Life ———— 56

Lesson 9 Varieties of Individuality ———— 62

Lesson 10 Loneliness ———— 70

Lesson 11 Poets and Poetry (1) ———— 75

Lesson 12 Poets and Poetry (2) ———— 82

Lesson 13 Settings of Love and Life ———— 88

Lesson 14 Imagination ———— 93

Lesson 15 America ———— 98

Lesson 1
American Lives and Loves

Word Power

Find the word's best definition and connect it to the word with a line.

mythic • • tough
rugged • • legendary
countless • • young girl or woman
maiden • • large area of flat, grassy land in North America
prairie • • many

commence • • requested (request)
mound • • a poem or song narrating a story in short groups of lines called stanzas
bade (bid) • • uncertain
obscure • • large rounded pile of soil at a grave
ballad • • begin

court • • feeling depressed
slight • • declare the punishment for
oppressed • • weapon like a knife with two sharp edges
dagger • • pursue someone you hope to marry
sentence • • insult

woe • • having saved money by not wasting it
gaily • • great sadness
villain • • kill
thrifty • • bad guy
slay • • in a happy way

Poem Reading 1

Cowboys have become mythic figures in American culture; they are portrayed as brave heroes of Western movies and emblems of rugged individualism. Cowboys have, in fact, become stereotypical representatives of the Unites States to other countries. Through the years, countless "cowboy songs" have been composed, sung, and recorded. Typically, these songs narrate the adventures of the men who drove cattle from the prairie lands to the markets. First recorded in 1929, "Cowboy Jack" was already a popular song among southern singers, but its true origin is lost in time. In any case, this sentimental song shares a universal theme of lost love.

Cowboy Jack
Anonymous

He was only just a cowboy,
But his heart was kind and true;
He'd won the heart of a maiden
With eyes of heaven's own blue.

They'd learned to love each other;
They'd named their wedding day,
When trouble came between them,
And the cowboy rode away.

He joined a band of cowboys,
To forget he tried to learn;
While out on the rolling prairie,
She waited for his return.

"Your sweetheart still waits for you, Jack,
Your sweetheart still waits for you
Way out on the rolling prairie,
Where the skies are always blue."

It was in a lonely cow camp,
Just at the close of day,
Someone said, "Sing a song, Jim,
That will drive all sorrows away."

When Jim commenced singing
Poor Jack's mind wandered back,
For the song told of a brave, true girl,
Who waited at home for Jack.

Poor Jack left camp next morning,
Breathing his sweetheart's name,
"I'll go and beg forgiveness,
For I know that I was to blame."

When he reached the rolling prairie,
He found a new-made mound.
The people kindly told him
They had laid his loved one down.

"In dying she spoke of you, Jack,
In dying she breathed your name.
She bade us with her last breath
To tell you when you came.

"With a heart that's breaking for you, Jack,
Your sweetheart still waits for you,
Way out on the rolling prairie
Where the skies are always blue."

Warm-up Activity

After you read the poem, choose the best words to fill in the blanks to complete the sentences.

Your sweetheart still _____ for you, Jack.

I'll go and _____ forgiveness because I know that I was _____ blame.

Jack, your sweetheart still waits _____ you on the prairie where the _____ are always blue.

| to skies beg for waits |

Questions

1. Do you think that this song describes a real cowboy's life? Or do you think this song describes a cowboy in an idealized or unrealistic fashion? Why?

2. When people say, "Your sweetheart still waits for you," where is the sweetheart actually waiting? Can you name the place "Where the skies are always blue"?

Poem Reading 2

"The Lily of the West" is based on a traditional Irish folk song. Its origins are obscure, but it has enjoyed popularity over the years, with versions recorded by Bob Dylan, Roseanne Cash, and the Chieftains, among many others. The story repeats a common theme in ballads: the main character commits a crime out of passion for his loved one.

The Lily of the West
Anonymous

I just came down from Louisville, some pleasure for to find;
A handsome girl from Michigan, so pleasing to my mind;
Her rosy cheeks and rolling eyes, like arrows, pierced my breast;
They call her handsome Mary—the Lily of the West.

Lesson 1   9

I courted her for many a day, her love I thought to gain;
Too soon, too soon she slighted me: which caused me grief and pain.
She robbed me of my liberty—deprived me of my rest;
They call her handsome Mary—the Lily of the West.

One evening, as I rambled down by yon shady grove,
I met a Lord of high degree, conversing with my love;
He sang, he sang so merrily, whilst I was sore oppressed,
He sang for handsome Mary—the Lily of the West.

I rushed up to my rival, a dagger in my hand,
I tore him from my true love, and boldly bade him stand;
Being mad to desperation, my dagger pierced his breast,
I was betrayed by Mary—the Lily of the West.

Now my trial has come on, and sentenced soon I'll be;
They put me in the criminal box, and there convicted me.
She so deceived the Jury, so modestly did dress,
She far outshine bright Venus—the Lily of the West.

Since then I've gained my liberty, I'll rove the country through;
I'll travel the city over, to find my loved one true;
Although she stole my liberty, and deprived me of my rest,
Still I love my Mary—the Lily of the West.

---

*oushine: 原文ではoutshineとなっているが、文法的にはoutshoneが正しい。

Warm-up Activity

After you read the poem, choose the best words to fill in the blanks to complete the sentences.

> I met a _____ girl from Michigan. I courted her for a long time and I thought I gained her _____ . However, I found a man of high social position _____ with my love. I _____ up to my rival with a _____ in my hand. My dagger _____ his chest. I was _____ in the criminal box, but she deceived the _____ by making herself look innocent, and making me alone seem guilty. After serving time in prison, I've gained my _____ , but I cannot _____ her.

| rushed put handsome jury forget dagger liberty conversing pierced love |

Questions

1. How does the narrator show his strong love for the girl?

2. Why is Mary attractive to the narrator? Choose three of Mary's characteristics that the narrator loves.

Poem Reading 3

"The Yellow Rose of Texas" is one of the most popular traditional American folk songs. Other folk songs have shared the term "rose" as a reference to a beloved woman. The earliest known publication of the song's lyrics in 1853 tells the story of an African American narrator who longs for his lover; "yellow" in this case refers to a mixed-race woman. Since the 1930s, the song's lyrics have been "racially neutral," rather than specifically referring to African American characters.

The Yellow Rose of Texas
Anonymous

There's a yellow rose of Texas that I am going to see,
No other fellow knows her, nobody else but me;
She cried so when I left her, it like to broke my heart,
And if I ever find her we never more will part.

Where the Rio Grande is flowing, and the starry skies are bright,
She walks along the river in the quiet summer night;
She thinks if I remember, when we parted long ago,
I promised to come back again, and not to leave her so.

Oh! Now I'm going to find her, for my heart is full of woe,
And we'll sing the song together, that we sung so long ago;
We'll play the banjo gaily, and we'll sing the songs of yore,
And the yellow rose of Texas shall be mine for evermore.

Warm-up Activity

After you read the poem, choose the best words to fill in the blanks to complete the sentences.

I am going to see a yellow rose _____ Texas. When I _____ her, she cried. I promised to come _____ again. Now I'm going _____ find her, and we'll _____ the song together.

sing   to   back   left   of

Questions

1. The narrator says the lovers will sing "the song of yore" when they meet again. Why will they sing an old song? What does the narrator imply with this hope?

2. Why does the narrator describe the separated condition of the lovers? Does the narrator really want to meet his love again? Is it truly possible for the narrator to possess the yellow rose of Texas forever?

Reading Challenge

Ellis Parker Butler (1869-1937) was a popular humorist who wrote many books and hundreds of stories for magazines. His fall from great popularity at the turn of the 20th century to near obscurity today shows that while his work entertained the readers of his day it has not endured the test of time. Parker's "Western" is a humorous ballad that parodies the sensationalized western stories that were popular with readers in the early 1900s.

Western
Ellis Parker Butler

The Cowboy had a sterling heart,
   The Maiden was from Boston,
The Rancher saw his wealth depart—
   The Steers were what he lost on.

The Villain was a banker's limb,
   His spats and cane were nifty;
The Maiden needs must marry him—
   Her father was not thrifty.

The Sheepmen were as foul as pitch,
   The Cowboy was a hero,
The gold mine made the hero rich,
   The Villain's score was zero.

The Sheepmen tried to steal the maid,
   The Villain sought the attic,
The Hero fifteen bad men slayed
   With his blue automatic.

The Hero kissed the willing lass,
   The final scene was snappy;
The Villain went to Boston, Mass.,
   And everyone was happy.

*needs must [=must needs] *do*: must *do* （ぜひともしなければならない）

Questions

1. The poem's situation is intentionally obscure. How many characters appear in this poem?

2. Create your own story from this poem. What happened in this poem? Why does the narrator present the story in this way?

Lesson 2
School Life in America

Word Power

Find the word's or the phrase's best definition and connect them with a line.

profound • • put up with
poignant • • monumentally important
landmark • • not based on any principle, plan, or system
arbitrary • • keen sadness
endure • • meaningfully deep

peremptory • • crush something until it becomes a fine powder
integer • • insistent, demanding something without explaining why
sheaves • • so as not to be separated
inseparably • • bundles of grain from the harvest
grind • • a whole number

ritual • • someone who knows a lot about a particular subject
dash off • • a child whose parents are dead
orphan • • write quickly
authority • • fundamental; basic
essential • • ceremony

robin • • extending its feathers
instructor • • sticking out
guess • • a small common bird which returns in the spring
overhanging • • a teacher, or someone who teaches a particular skill
ruffling • • suppose; think

Poem Reading 1

Howard Nemerov (1920-1991) was born in New York City, the son of Russian Jews who owned a famous Fifth Avenue department store. After graduating from Harvard he began a career as a poet, novelist, essayist, and university teacher. Librarian of Congress James Billington remarked that Nemerov's subject matter ranges "from the profound to the poignant to the comic." Nemerov twice served as United States poet laureate and won a Pulitzer Prize in 1978 for his *Collected Poems*. The first day of school is a landmark event for most children and their parents. Nemerov explores the changes in life associated with this "ritual" and hopes for the best.

＊poet laureate = a poet holding an honorary representative position in a country（桂冠詩人）

September, the First Day of School
Howard Nemerov

I

My child and I hold hands on the way to school,
And when I leave him at the first-grade door
He cries a little but is brave; he does
Let go. My selfish tears remember how
I cried before that door a life ago.
I may have had a hard time letting go.

Each fall the children must endure together
What each child also must endure alone:
Learning the alphabet, the integers,
Three dozen bits and pieces of a stuff
So arbitrary, so peremptory,
That worlds invisible and visible

Bow down before it, as in Joseph's dream
The sheaves bowed down and then the stars bowed down
Before the dreaming of a little boy.
That dream got him such hatred of his brothers
As cost the greater part of life to mend,
And yet great kindness came of it in the end.

II

A school is where they grind the grain of thought,
And grind the children who must mind the thought.
It may be those two grindings are but one,
As from the alphabet come Shakespeare's Plays,
As from the integers comes Euler's Law,
As from the whole, inseparably, the lives,

The shrunken lives that have not been set free
By law or by poetic fantasy.
But may they be. My child has disappeared
Behind the schoolroom door. And should I live
To see his coming forth, a life away,
I know my hope, but do not know its form

Nor hope to know it. May the fathers he finds
Among his teachers have a care of him
More than his father could. How that will look
I do not know, I do not need to know.
Even our tears belong to ritual.
But may great kindness come of it in the end.

Warm-up Activity

After you read the poem, choose the best words to fill in the blanks to complete the sentences.

> On the _____ day of school, my child and I hold _____ and go to _____ . He cries a _____ but bravely goes to the classroom. My child has _____ behind the schoolroom door. I hope he finds _____ teachers who will take care of him more _____ _____ _____ _____ .

hands	than	little	father	first	school	his	could	disappeared	good

Questions

1. What kind of memories come to the father when he is taking his son to school? What kind of differences does he find between himself and his child?

2. What kind of lessons will the poet's son have in school? What does he think about his son's future?

Poem Reading 2

Frank O'Hara (1926-1966) was an American writer, poet, and art critic. He served as a curator at the Museum of Modern Art and was sometimes referred to as "a poet among painters." A leading figure of the New York School, O'Hara often dashed off poems in a natural, casual way, including bits of conversation and everyday references. He wrote "Autobiographia Literaria" when he was a student at Harvard. In writing this poem, O'Hara might have found a reward for all of the lonesome days of his childhood.

Autobiographia Literaria
Frank O'Hara

When I was a child
I played by myself in a
corner of the schoolyard
all alone.

I hated dolls and I
hated games, animals were
not friendly and birds
flew away.

If anyone was looking
for me I hid behind a
tree and cried out "I am
an orphan."

And here I am, the
center of all beauty!
writing these poems!
Imagine!

Warm-up Activity

After you read the poem, choose the best words to fill in the blanks to complete the sentences.

When I _____ a child I played _____ myself in a _____ of the schoolyard. I hated playing with dolls and I hated _____ with friends. If anyone was looking _____ me, I _____ _____ a tree. But now I am writing these poems in the _____ of _____ _____. How wonderful!

center   behind   all   games   by   hid   beauty   corner   was   for

Questions

1. What kind of activities did the other children do when the poet was a child?

2. This is a poem about becoming a poet. According to this poem, what kind of experience is important for the poet?

Lesson 2   17

Poem Reading 3

Mary Ruefle (1952-) is an American poet, fiction writer, and teacher. Her free-verse poetry can appear to be light and fun, yet at the same time somber and profound. Ruefle's inventive and haunting style is evident in *A Little White Shadow* (2006), in which she creates meaning by erasing all but a few words from various texts. In "The Hand," Ruefle isolates the common gesture of the classroom when students raise their hand to answer a question the teacher has posed to the class.

The Hand
Mary Ruefle

The teacher asks a question.
You know the answer, you suspect
you are the only one in the classroom
who knows the answer, because the person
in question is yourself, and on that
you are the greatest living authority,
but you don't raise your hand.
You raise the top of your desk
and take out an apple.
You look out the window.

You don't raise your hand and there is
some essential beauty in your fingers,
which aren't even drumming, but lie
flat and peaceful.
The teacher repeats the question.
Outside the window, on an overhanging
  branch,
a robin is ruffling its feathers
and spring is in the air.

Warm-up Activity

After you read the poem, choose the best words to fill in the blanks to complete the sentences.

> The teacher asks a _____ . You know the _____ . You feel you are the _____ one in the _____ who knows the answer, but you don't _____ your hand. Instead, you raise the _____ of your desk and take _____ an apple. You look out the _____ . Outside the window, _____ is _____ the air.

window top only classroom question raise spring out in answer

Questions

1. This poem describes the situation in which the teacher asks a question and you know the answer, but you do not raise your hand. Did you ever have such an experience in school? Why did you not raise your hand? What is the difference between knowing the answer and raising your hand?

2. Notice the contrast in the last stage of this poem: the classroom and the outside. What kind of contrast does the poem suggest about these two worlds?

Reading Challenge

Langston Hughes (1902-1967) was an American poet, social activist, novelist, and playwright, and is regarded as an influential leader of the Harlem Renaissance of the 1920s. Hughes wrote in everyday language about the everyday lives of African Americans. He grew up in Joplin, Missouri, where he was one of only two African American students in his high school class. When he attended Columbia University in 1921, he was one of only a dozen African American students on campus. Reflecting on his educational experiences years later, Hughes wrote "Theme for English B."

Theme for English B
Langston Hughes

The instructor said,

*Go home and write
a page tonight.
And let that page come out of you—
Then, it will be true.*

I wonder if it's that simple?
I am twenty-two, colored, born in Winston-Salem.
I went to school there, then Durham, then here
to this college on the hill above Harlem.
I am the only colored student in my class.
The steps from the hill lead down into Harlem,
through a park, then I cross St. Nicholas,
Eighth Avenue, Seventh, and I come to the Y,
the Harlem Branch Y, where I take the elevator
up to my room, sit down, and write this page:

It's not easy to know what is true for you or me

at twenty-two, my age. But I guess I'm what
I feel and see and hear, Harlem, I hear you:
hear you, hear me—we two—you, me, talk on this page.
(I hear New York, too.) Me—who?
Well, I like to eat, sleep, drink, and be in love.
I like to work, read, learn, and understand life.
I like a pipe for a Christmas present,
or records—Bessie, bop, or Bach.
I guess being colored doesn't make me *not* like
the same things other folks like who are other races.
So will my page be colored that I write?
Being me, it will not be white.
But it will be
a part of you, instructor.
You are white—
yet a part of me, as I am a part of you.
That's American.
Sometimes perhaps you don't want to be a part of me.
Nor do I often want to be a part of you.
But we are, that's true!
As I learn from you,
I guess you learn from me—
although you're older—and white—
and somewhat more free.

This is my page for English B.

---

*The Harlem Branch Y = The Harlem branch of the YMCA (the YMCA is known for renting inexpensive rooms for a short stay).

Questions

1. What is the instructor's intention? What kind of writing does the instructor expect from the student? Why does the poet think the instructor's direction is difficult to follow?

2. What kind of social condition does the poet call attention to in this poem?

Lesson 3
Mother

Word Power

Find the word's best definition and connect it to the word with a line.

clergyman • • a religious song or poem
temptation • • inviting someone to believe something that is not true
hymn • • wait
deceptive • • desire for something bad
linger • • priest or minister

biographer • • patience
invoke • • a person who writes someone's life
endurance • • a clear transparent mineral
crystal • • a small, sharp nail
tack • • call earnestly for

splinter • • lineal descent from an ancestor
celebrate • • a small, thin, sharp piece of wood
mythic • • children
lineage • • praise
progeny • • legendary

vital • • repress
trudge • • force someone to do something
smother • • a burning stick used as a guiding light
torch • • very important
impel • • walk slowly because of exhaustion or harsh conditions

21

Poem Reading 1

Jones Very (1813–1880) was an American poet, essayist, clergyman, and mystic. He studied the work of William Shakespeare so intently that he wrote mostly Shakespearean sonnets. Very's friend Ralph Waldo Emerson and other American Transcendentalists recognized the high quality of his poetry and criticism. The speaker in this poem recalls his mother's voice from various childhood events: suffering an illness, learning about religion, and avoiding temptation.

＊mystic ＝ 神秘主義者　＊Shakespearean sonnets ＝ シェイクスピア風の14行詩　＊Transcendentalists ＝ 超絶主義者

My Mother's Voice
Jones Very

My mother's voice!　I hear it now,
I feel her hand upon my brow,
　　As when in heartfelt joy
She raised her evening hymn of praise,
And called down blessings on the days
　　Of her loved boy.

My mother's voice!　I hear it now,
Her hand is on my burning brow,
　　As in that early hour
When fever throbbed through all my veins,
And that fond hand first soothed my pains
　　With healing power.

My mother's voice!　It sounds as when
She read to me of holy men,
　　The Patriarchs of old:
And, gazing downward on my face,
She seemed each infant thought to trace
　　My young eyes told.

It comes — when thoughts unhallowed throng
Woven in sweet deceptive song —
　　And whispers round my heart;
As when at eve it rose on high,
I hear and think that she is nigh,
　　And they depart.

Though round my heart all, all beside,
The voice of Friendship, Love, had died,
　　That voice would linger there;
As when, soft pillowed on her breast,
Its tones first lulled my infant rest
　　Or rose in prayer.

Warm-up Activity

After you read the poem, choose the best words to fill in the blanks to complete the sentences.

I still hear my mother's _____ now. When in heartfelt joy, she sang her evening _____ of praise, and asked for God's blessings on her boy. When _____ ran through all my veins, her hand was on my _____ brow. Her fond hand soothed my pains with _____ power. When thoughts unhallowed throng woven in sweet _____ song, my mother's voice comes again and _____ to my heart. Though the voice of _____ and love had died in my heart, my mother's voice would _____ there in the same way as it did when its tones first quieted my _____ sleep.

| whispers   linger   infant   burning   voice   healing   fever   deceptive   hymn   friendship |

Questions

1. Is the mother's voice a real one? Or does the poet just imagine that he is listening to the mother's voice?

2. Why does he still demand his mother's voice? What does the poet's desire suggest about his condition?

Poem Reading 2

In his early poems, Langston Hughes created a new approach for an American poet. According to biographer Arnold Rampersad, Hughes sought to establish in poetry a new "tradition according to the standards of a group often seen as sub-poetic – the black masses." In "Mother to Son," written in 1923, Rampersad explains that Hughes welcomed the common voice of black people into poetry, invoking their "courage, endurance, and sense of duty."

Mother to Son
Langston Hughes

Well, son, I'll tell you:
Life for me ain't been no crystal stair.
It's had tacks in it,
And splinters,
And boards torn up,
And places with no carpet on the floor—
Bare.
But all the time
I'se been a-climbin' on,
And reachin' landin's,
And turnin' corners,
And sometimes goin' in the dark
Where there ain't been no light.
So boy, don't you turn back.
Don't you set down on the steps
'Cause you finds it's kinder hard.
Don't you fall now—
For I'se still goin', honey,
I'se still climbin',
And life for me ain't been no crystal stair.

Lesson 3

Warm-up Activity

After you read the poem, choose the best words to fill in the blanks to complete the sentences.

> Well, son, I tell you that my _____ has not been _____ stairs. My life has been a _____ process. It has had painful tacks and _____ . But I've been climbing up the _____ . Sometimes I was moving in the _____ , where there was no light. Therefore, boy, don't turn _____ . Don't _____ down on the steps even if you feel it is hard to _____ . I've also been _____ up these difficult stairs.

crystal back steps life climbing splinters dark sit difficult climb

Questions

1. How is this mother's voice different from the one in Jones Very's "My Mother's Voice"? What kind of power does the mother's voice have in Langston Hughes' "Mother to Son"?

....

....

....

2. What kinds of images does the mother's voice offer to the poet? How are these images related to the mother's life, or the poet's?

....

....

....

Reading Challenge

In this poem, Hughes celebrates the power of the mythic mother of "Negro" people. In her voice, Hughes delivers a speech that traces the lineage of slavery from Africa to the United States. Drawing on religious symbols of light and dark, the mother urges her progeny to take the next vital steps toward freedom.

The Negro Mother
Langston Hughes

Children, I come back today
To tell you a story of the long dark way
That I had to climb, that I had to know
In order that the race might live and grow.
Look at my face—dark as the night—
Yet shining like the sun with love's true light.
I am the child they stole from the sand
Three hundred years ago in Africa's land.
I am the dark girl who crossed the wide sea
Carrying in my body the seed of the free.
I am the woman who worked in the field
Bringing the cotton and the corn to yield.
I am the one who labored as a slave,
Beaten and mistreated for the work that I gave—
Children sold away from me, husband sold, too.
No safety, no love, no respect was I due.
Three hundred years in the deepest South:
But God put a song and a prayer in my mouth.
God put a dream like steel in my soul.
Now, through my children, I'm reaching the goal.
Now, through my children, young and free,
I realize the blessings denied to me.
I couldn't read then. I couldn't write.
I had nothing, back there in the night.
Sometimes, the valley was filled with tears,
But I kept trudging on through the lonely years.
Sometimes, the road was hot with sun,
But I had to keep on till my work was done:
I *had* to keep on! No stopping for me—
I was the seed of the coming Free.
I nourished the dream that nothing could smother
Deep in my breast—the Negro mother.
I had only hope then, but now through you,
Dark ones of today, my dreams must come true:
All you dark children in the world out there,
Remember my sweat, my pain, my despair.
Remember my years, heavy with sorrow—
And make of those years a torch for tomorrow.
Make of my past a road to the light
Out of the darkness, the ignorance, the night.
Lift high my banner out of the dust.
Stand like free men supporting my trust.
Believe in the right, let none push you back.
Remember the whip and the slaver's track.
Remember how the strong in struggle and strife
Still bar you the way, and deny you life—
But march ever forward, breaking down bars.
Look ever upward at the sun and the stars.
Oh, my dark children, may my dreams and my prayers
Impel you forever up the great stairs—
For I will be with you till no white brother
Dares keep down the children of the Negro mother.

Warm-up Activity

After you read the poem, choose the best words to fill in the blanks to complete the sentences.

My children should know my history in order for the race to live and _____ in the future. White people brought me from Africa three _____ years ago. I worked in the _____ bringing _____ and corn to harvest. I labored as a _____ , and I was beaten and _____ while I was working. But God put a dream like steel in my _____ . I nourished the _____ that nothing could smother deep in my heart. All African American children in the world should remember my sweat, my _____ , my despair, to make of those years a _____ for tomorrow.

> fields soul grow torch pain slave mistreated dream cotton hundred

Questions

1. In the first line of this poem, the mother's voice says, "I come back today." Can you imagine from where this mother comes back? Why?

2. What does this mother's voice want to tell the children?

Guide 1

What can you do with a poem? Perform it!

What if you don't know what to do with a poem? There the poem is, sitting on the page doing nothing. Boring words once written by some person who is now dead and gone. But those words are only boring until they are spoken, until they are heard, and an easy first step with any poem is to try to read it out loud. To speak even a small part of it out loud can bring it to life, and if we can speak from the heart—perform the poem—then sometimes an amazing thing happens: we and our listeners can feel the deep emotions in another person's voice.

When you hear your favorite song, it affects you strongly, doesn't it? Perhaps it makes you want to move your body, to dance, or maybe it makes you think of a person you love. Why? Because someone is performing a poem so well that it speaks to you powerfully. Since you are probably a beginner, maybe your version of a song or poem will not be so perfect, but it still will be much better than leaving the words sitting silently on the page.

Also, if the poem is in a foreign language then you will have a great chance to practice your skills in pronouncing sounds, or using effective intonation or pauses. Take a look at this example, a short poem by Emily Dickinson.

> To make a prairie it takes a clover and one bee,
> One clover, and a bee,
> And revery.
> The revery alone will do,
> If bees are few.

That's it. The whole poem. Just five short lines that tell about how to "make a prairie," which seems like a pretty tough thing to do, actually. The poem gives a sort of "recipe" for creating a prairie, and the ingredients are just a bee and a clover—and some "revery," that is, some imagination. The humorous ending even suggests that just one ingredient is enough, if it is imagination. A simple, funny poem about the power of imagination.

But what if you want to perform it? Perfect, isn't it. It is short, and it even repeats many of the same words, so memorizing it is easy. If you are a native speaker of Japanese, however, the tough part—and the useful part—is that the poem has many "r" and "l" sounds. First, break the poem into even smaller parts, like this:

> To make a prairie
> it takes a clover
> and one bee,
> One clover,
> and a bee,
> And revery.
> The revery alone will do,
> If bees are few.

Then practice it a few times, line by line, maybe with some feedback from your teacher. Soon, you will have improved your English pronunciation, but you will also have a precious possession: a poem you can perform that will make you smile, and others too, if you like.

Lesson 3

Lesson 4
Love (1)

W o r d   P o w e r

Find the word's or the phrase's best definition and connect them with a line.

derive   •   • a small hollow in someone's face, often seen when they smile
dialogue   •   • descend
bid   •   • request
dimple   •   • curls in one's hair
ringlets   •   • conversation

involve   •   • important status
intend   •   • a great respect
tribute   •   • include
grand stature   •   • praise
a high regard   •   • plan

musket   •   • a person whose job is to make or mend shoes
haberdasher   •   • a person whose job is to make men's clothes
tailor   •   • praise
cobbler   •   • an early type of gun with a long barrel
hail   •   • a shop where men's clothes are sold

curse   •   • a person's manner in walking
gait   •   • change
alter   •   • an utterance intended to harm someone
stubble   •   • soft
tender   •   • short stalks standing in fields after corn or wheat has been cut

28

Poem Reading 1

"Billy Boy" is a folk song and nursery rhyme that likely derives from "Lord Randal," a traditional ballad that dates back to the 1600s. "Lord Randal" relates a tragic dialogue between a mother and her son as he tells her that he has murdered his lover after she poisoned him. While similar in its mother-and-son dialogue structure, "Billy Boy" is a happier story suitable for children.

Billy Boy
Anonymous

Oh, where have you been, Billy boy, Billy boy?
Oh, where have you been, charming Billy?
I have been to seek a wife, she's the joy of my life;
   She's a young thing, and cannot leave her mother.

Did she bid you to come in, Billy boy, Billy boy?
Did she bid you to come in, charming Billy?
Yes, she bade me to come in, there's a dimple in her chin.
   She's a young thing, and cannot leave her mother.

Did she set for you a chair, Billy boy, Billy boy?
Did she set for you a chair, charming Billy?
Yes, she sat for me a chair, she has ringlets in her hair.
   She's a young thing, and cannot leave her mother.

Can she make a cherry pie, Billy boy, Billy boy?
Can she make a cherry pie, charming Billy?
She can make a cherry pie, quick as a cat can wink her eye.
   She's a young thing, and cannot leave her mother.

How old is she, Billy boy, Billy boy?
How old is she, charming Billy?
She's three times six, four times seven, twenty-eight and eleven.
   She's a young thing, and cannot leave her mother.

Warm-up Activity

After you read the poem, choose the best words to fill in the blanks to complete the sentences.

Where _____ you been, Billy boy?

I have been to _____ a wife.

Did she _____ you to _____ in, Billy boy?

Yes, she _____ me to come in, there's a _____ in her chin.

Lesson 4   29

Can she make a _____ pie, Billy boy?

She can make a cherry pie, quick as a cat can _____ her eye.

How _____ is she, Billy boy?

She's three times six, four _____ seven, twenty-eight and eleven.

seek old times wink cherry come bade dimple bid have

Questions

1. This is a simple nursery rhyme. In what situation can you imagine this nursery rhyme will be recited?

2. Can you calculate the woman's age, when Billy Boy says, "She's three times six, four times seven, twenty-eight and eleven"?

Poem Reading 2

Many variations of this song have been written down and recorded in the past hundred years, and undoubtedly the song is older than that. This dialogue song has many variations, yet always involves a young woman and a soldier she loves. While this song may have originally been intended as a tribute to the grand stature of soldiers, today we might read it as a warning to young women not to hold a man in too high a regard.

Soldier, Soldier Will You Marry Me
Anonymous

Soldier, soldier will you marry me,
With your musket, fife and drum?
Oh, how can I marry such a pretty girl as you,
When I have no hat to put on?
Off to the haberdasher she did go, as fast as
    she could run,
Bought him a hat, the best that was there,
And the soldier put it on.

Soldier, soldier will you marry me,
With your musket, fife and drum?
Oh, how can I marry such a pretty girl as you,
When I have no coat to put on?
Off to the tailor she did go, as fast as
    she could run,
Bought him a coat, the best that was there,
And the soldier put it on.

Soldier, soldier will you marry me,
With your musket, fife and drum?
Oh, how can I marry such a pretty girl as you,
When I have no boots to put on?
Off to the cobbler she did go, as fast as
    she could run,
Bought him a pair of the best that was there,
And the soldier put them on.

Soldier, soldier will you marry me,
With your musket, fife and drum?
Oh, how can I marry such a pretty girl as you,
When I have no pants to put on?
Off to the tailor she did go, as fast as
    she could run,
Bought him a pair, the best that was there,
And the soldier put them on.

Now soldier, soldier will you marry me,
With your musket, fife and drum?
Well, how can I marry such a pretty girl as
    you,
With a wife and three kids back home?

Warm-up Activity

After you read the poem, choose the best words to fill in the blanks to complete the sentences

Soldier, _____ , will you _____ me?

Oh, how _____ I marry such a pretty girl _____ you,
When I have _____ hat, no coat, no pants to _____ on?

I bring _____ a hat, a coat, and a _____ of pants. Now, soldier, soldier, will you marry me?

Well, how can I marry such _____ pretty girl as you, with a wife and three _____ back home?

| kids | no | marry | a | put | as | pair | can | soldier | you |

Lesson 4   31

Questions

1. This is a duet between a young girl and a soldier. What is the message of this song?

2. In the last stanza, the soldier confesses that he has a wife and three kids. Why does the soldier wait to tell this important information?

Poem Reading 3

Dorothy Parker (1893-1967) was an American poet, writer, and critic famous for her sharp wit. Gaining positions as editor at magazines such as *Vogue*, then at *Vanity Fair* and *The New Yorker*, Parker was remarkably successful at a young age, particularly for a woman at a time when most editing posts in the top magazines went to men. Harpo Marx, Ernest Hemingway, and F. Scott Fitzgerald were among the many luminaries who considered Parker as a friend. In this poem, the speaker addresses women and warns them of the ways that men charm women while they intend to change them.

Men
Dorothy Parker

They hail you as their morning star
Because you are the way you are.
If you return the sentiment,
They'll try to make you different;
And once they have you, safe and sound,
They want to change you all around.
Your moods and ways they put a curse on;
They'd make of you another person.
They cannot let you go your gait;
They influence and educate.
They'd alter all that they admired.
They make me sick, they make me tired.

Warm-up Activity

After you read the poem, choose the best words to fill in the blanks to complete the sentences.

> Men at first _____ you because you are what you are. However, _____ you return your love to them, they want to _____ you as they wish. They want to make you _____ person. Such men make me _____, and make me tired.

change once sick admire another

Questions

1. Can you guess the reason for the changes of men's attitudes to a woman? Why would they wish to alter that which they admired?

_____

_____

_____

2. What kind of woman do the men in this poem demand?

_____

_____

_____

Poem Reading 4

Ogden Nash (1902-1971) was a rarity among American poets: a writer of light verse who achieved highly regarded artistic success. "During his lifetime," according to the *Poetry Foundation*, "Ogden Nash was the most widely known, appreciated, and imitated American creator of light verse, a reputation that has continued after his death." However, in addition to his many humorous short verses, such as "Reflections on Ice Breaking," Nash was also a Hollywood screenwriter, a children's book writer, a regular radio and TV show guest, and the lyricist for a smash hit Broadway musical, *One Touch of Venus*, in 1943. He remains best known for his ability to portray odd human weaknesses in humorous short verse. In this one, Nash offers advice on the best way to start a conversation – or to speed up romance.

Lesson 4 33

Reflections on Ice-Breaking
Ogden Nash

Candy
Is dandy
But liquor
Is quicker.

Warm-up Activity

After you read the poem, choose the best words to fill in the blanks to complete the sentences.

Offering candy ____ ____ ____ ____ ____ ____ start a communication, but liquor is ____ ____ ____ ____ become intimate in conversation.

| nice a is very way to / way faster the to |

Questions

1. This is a humorous short poem. Candy is a good gift when you wish to get to know someone, but alcohol will work more quickly. Also, a person can use alcohol to convince someone to do something. Can you connect this poem with the previous poem, Dorothy Parker's "Men"? What does Nash's poem suggest about some men's character?

2. What does "Ice-Breaking" mean? How is this theme connected to the theme of love?

Reading Challenge

Stephen Crane (1871-1900) was an American poet, novelist, and short story writer who remains best known for his novel, *The Red Badge of Courage* (1895), which is frequently assigned to students in high schools and universities. Crane also published poems (he referred to them simply as "lines") that prefigured the style and thematic content of much modern poetry. His use in this poem of a dialogue – without identifying either of the speakers – and his lack of rhyme or formal structure are typical of his sparse, dry lines.

And You Love Me?
Stephen Crane

And you love me?

I love you.

You are, then, cold coward.

Aye; but, beloved,
When I strive to come to you,
Man's opinions, a thousand thickets,
My interwoven existence,
My life,
Caught in the stubble of the world
Like a tender veil, —
This stays me.
No strange move can I make
Without noise of tearing.
I dare not.

If love loves,
There is no world
Nor word.
All is lost
Save thought of love
And place to dream.
You love me?

I love you.

You are, then, cold coward.

Aye; but, beloved—

Questions

1. **This poem may be read as a conversation between a woman and a man. Describe their situation.**

2. **When the woman says "If love loves, / There is no world / Nor word," what does the woman suggest? What does the man need to do to satisfy the woman?**

Lesson 4 35

Lesson 5
Love (2)

W o r d   P o w e r

Find the word's or the phrase's best definition and connect them with a line.

hobo •	• excessively
freight train •	• not damaged or marked in any way; perfect
overly •	• a homeless, travelling worker
unblemished •	• connect
associate •	• a railroad car carrying goods
bushel •	• a branch of mathematics
arithmetic •	• begin
measure •	• keen; accurate
insightful •	• estimate
initiate •	• a unit of capacity equal to 35.2 liters, used for grains, fruits, etc.
breakup •	• religious songs
brittle •	• included
incorporated •	• imitate
spirituals •	• delicate and fragile
mimic •	• an end to a relationship
courtly •	• joyful
jubilant •	• formal, traditional
roaming •	• sweet smell; perfume
fragrance •	• the near future
morrow •	• wandering

Poem Reading 1

Carl Sandburg (1878 – 1967) was an American poet, writer, and collector of folk songs. Sandburg left school at a young age and traveled widely as a hobo, riding freight trains. Sandburg's poetry, based on a free-verse style of everyday speech, influenced poets such as Langston Hughes. For many readers Sandburg's poetry seemed overly simple and unpoetic, while for others his poetry presented fresh, clearly stated, unblemished images of America. In this poem, for example, Sandburg uses words associated with the marketplace to emphasize that measurements of love, like those of the marketplace or the weather, can change from day to day.

*free verse= poetry that does not rhyme or have a regular meter (定型の韻律に縛られない自由詩)

How Much?
Carl Sandburg

How much do you love me, a million bushels?
Oh, a lot more than that, Oh, a lot more.

And to-morrow maybe only half a bushel?
To-morrow maybe not even a half a bushel.

And is this your heart arithmetic?
This is the way the wind measures the weather.

Warm-up Activity

After you read the poem, choose the best words to fill in the blanks to complete the sentences

How _____ do you love me?

Oh, I love you a _____ .

And _____ , your love _____ by _____ ?

Tomorrow, perhaps my love declines more _____ half.

How do you predict your _____ ?

I _____ my heart with my own moods, in the way the _____ measures the _____ .

> lot declines wind emotion much weather measure half than tomorrow

Questions

1. This poem seems to be a conversation between two people. What kind of relationship do they have? Are they young or old? Why do you think so?

2. "A woman's mind and winter wind change often," a proverb says. Why does one person in this poem compare the human heart to the weather in the same way as the proverb does? What does this poem, or the proverb, suggest about the heart?

Poem Reading 2

Although Dorothy Parker gained fame for her poems that were often laced with irony and insightful humor, she also knew a darker side of life. She suffered her share of emotional difficulties, particularly in the 1920s when she experienced several painful love affairs. This poem recognizes that a breakup can cause pain to the heartbroken one and also to the one who initiated the breakup.

A Very Short Song
Dorothy Parker

Once, when I was young and true,
  Someone left me sad—
Broke my brittle heart in two;
  And that is very bad.

Love is for unlucky folk,
  Love is but a curse.
Once there was a heart I broke;
  And that, I think, is worse.

Warm-up Activity

After you read the poem, choose the best words to fill in the blanks to complete the sentences.

When I _____ young and _____ , a man _____ my heart in _____ and that was a very _____ experience. I think _____ is only a _____ . Once _____ broke a man's _____ , and that experience was _____ .

true I broke heart worse was two curse bad love

Questions

1. Why does the poet think that breaking another's heart is worse than having the poet's own heart broken?

2. Why does the poet think love is a curse?

Poem Reading 3

Langston Hughes knew about the importance of songs. One of his breakthrough poems was "The Weary Blues," about an elderly blues singer; the poem even incorporated some blues-style lyrics, for the first time in American poetry. Hughes referred to "song" in many of his poems, and used the word "song" in many titles. Hughes felt the power of voice in the African American's work songs, spirituals, and blues, and sought to build that voice into his poetry. In this poem, he seems to summon the power of song that is beyond words. The act of singing – even the desire to sing to another – may be enough to communicate.

Lesson 5   39

Songs
Langston Hughes

I sat there singing her
Songs in the dark.

She said,
I do not understand
The words.

I said,
There are
No words.

Warm-up Activity

After you read the poem, choose the best words to fill in the blanks to complete the sentences.

_____ am _____ songs _____ the _____ .

I cannot _____ your _____ .

My songs are _____ telling the _____ of words, but _____ my _____ .

| telling   intention   understand   meaning   in   words   I   not   dark   singing |

Questions

1. The narrator might be a man who sings songs for his lover. In what way can you connect this poem with Stephen Crane's "And You Love Me"? What is the narrator's intention when he says, "There are / no words"?

2. In this poem, the woman wants to know the meaning of words but the narrator isn't concerned about the words. What is the message of this poem?

Reading Challenge

Dorothy Parker's song here is quite different from Hughes's song. While Hughes shows the capacity of a song to reach someone even without words, Parker uses her words to create a distance between her and her ironically referred-to "love." The first seven lines of each stanza mimic traditional courtly poetry, the kind that might have been written by a Shakespeare-era sonneteer, while the final line in each stanza spins an unexpected reversal.

Love Song
Dorothy Parker

My own dear love, he is strong and bold
    And he cares not what comes after.
His words ring sweet as a chime of gold,
    And his eyes are lit with laughter.
He is jubilant as a flag unfurled—
    Oh, a girl, she'd not forget him.
My own dear love, he is all my world—
    And I wish I'd never met him.

My love, he's mad, and my love, he's fleet,
    And a wild young wood-thing bore him!
The ways are fair to his roaming feet,
    And the skies are sunlit for him.
As sharply sweet to my heart he seems
    As the fragrance of acacia.
My own dear love, he is all my dreams—
    And I wish he were in Asia.

My love runs by like a day in June,
    And he makes no friends of sorrows.
He'll tread his galloping rigadoon
    In the pathway of the morrows.
He'll live his days where the sunbeams start,
    Nor could storm or wind uproot him.
My own dear love, he is all my heart—
    And I wish somebody'd shoot him.

*rigadoon: リゴドン、4分の2拍子または4分の4拍子の快活な踊り。この詩では、馬が快活に走る様子の比喩として用いられている。

Warm-up Activity

After you read the poem, choose the best words to fill in the blanks to complete the sentences.

My sweetheart is strong and _____ . His words _____ sweet. He is jubilant. My sweetheart is _____ my world, and I wish I had _____ met him. My sweetheart seems as _____ as the fragrance of _____ to my heart. My sweetheart is all my dreams, and I wish he _____ in Asia. My love does not continue being _____ for a long time. He will live in a hopeful place. My love, he is all my _____ , and I wish somebody would _____ him.

ring   shoot   were   bold   sad   acacia   all   sweet   never   heart

Questions

1. Could you find the positive elements of the man's character? Find some words that suggest the amicable elements of the narrator's lover.

2. Why does she wish he were in Asia? Why do you think she wishes somebody would shoot him? Can you connect the last line of this poem with Dorothy Parker's "Men"?

Lesson 6

Suicide, Sickness, and Death

Word Power

Find the word's best definition and connect it to the word with a line.

blues • • the words of a poem or song
lyrics • • abandon
suicide • • a group of lines in a poem
stanza • • the act of killing oneself intentionally
desert • • sad music of black American folk origin

allude to • • rainstorm
deluge • • refer to
note • • testing
experimenting • • always
consistently • • a short message

recognition • • quality or characteristic
bygone • • past
attribute • • dressed
pavement • • appreciation
arrayed • • street or sidewalk

grace • • smallest units of living things
nominate • • courageous
cells • • smallest pieces of non-living things; atoms
particles • • elegance
undaunted • • select

43

Poem Reading 1

In 1926 Hughes published a poem in *Poetry* magazine titled "Suicide." This poem was in the form of a blues lyric, in which a line is delivered and then repeated; the third and final line of the stanza usually rhymes with the first two lines and adds a twist of meaning. The narrator in that poem is a woman who has been deserted by the man she loved, and she hopes to find peace in the river's water, where "a po', po' gal can sleep" ["poor, poor girl"]. "Suicide's Note," published a year before "Suicide," provides no explanation for the speaker's (or in the case of this "Suicide's Note," the writer's) reason for wishing to die, beyond the suggestion that calmness awaits.

Suicide's Note
Langston Hughes

The calm,
Cool face of the river
Asked me for a kiss.

Warm-up Activity

Read the poem, and then arrange the words to complete the sentences.

The river's face was calm and cool. This face _____ _____ _____ _____ _____ . So _____ _____ _____ _____ _____ died.

me a for kiss asked / kissed and face the I

Questions

1. **What kind of emotion do you feel in this poem? If you feel this poem is humorous, what elements will give you that feeling?**

2. **The narrator seems to leave this "Suicide's Note" and drown himself in the river. How does this poem communicate its image of death?**

Poem Reading 2

Langston Hughes writes one sentence here, focused on the initial phrase, "how quiet." The word "sheet" alludes to a cotton bed sheet, but the word can also mean a blinding deluge, as in "sheets of rain." As with his poem "Songs" above, Hughes lets the suspended scene speak for itself. He offers no comment except to note that due to the woman's illness, she may die.

Sick Room
Langston Hughes

How quiet
It is in this sick room
Where on the bed
A silent woman lies between two lovers—
Life and Death,
And all three covered with a sheet of pain.

Warm-up Activity

Read the poem, and then arrange the words to complete the sentences.

This sick room is quiet. A silent _____ _____ _____ _____ _____. She has two lovers, life and death. All three are _____ _____ _____ _____ _____ _____ pain.

| the woman on lies bed / of a covered sheet with |

Questions

1. Why does the poet imagine Life and Death as "two lovers"? Do both Life and Death love the sick woman? What do they want to do? Is this a shocking poem?

2. Why does a "sheet of pain" cover "all three"? Who is feeling pain?

Lesson 6   45

Poem Reading 3

While most poets after the turn of the 20th Century seemed to be experimenting with verse forms, including free verse, Edwin Arlington Robinson (1869-1935) remained consistently a poet of traditional verse forms. Robinson often wrote of people who failed and people who longed for a past time. This is not surprising as Robinson was personally familiar with struggling for recognition as a poet as well as for writing in a style that seemed better suited to bygone days. In 1897, Robinson published a book of poems titled *Children of the Night*. President Theodore Roosevelt's son admired the book and shared it with his father who not only recommended to a big-name publisher that they print it, but he also wrote a review for it. This book contains Robinson's poem "Richard Cory," which remains one of his best-known works. Richard Cory represents the attributes we typically associate with success: good looks, money, and a smooth manner. It is natural that we might be jealous of such a person.

Richard Cory
Edwin Arlington Robinson

Whenever Richard Cory went down town,
We people on the pavement looked at him:
He was a gentleman from sole to crown,
Clean favored, and imperially slim.

And he was always quietly arrayed,
And he was always human when he talked;
But still he fluttered pulses when he said,
"Good-morning," and he glittered when he walked.

And he was rich—yes, richer than a king—
And admirably schooled in every grace:
In fine, we thought that he was everything
To make us wish that we were in his place.

So on we worked, and waited for the light,
And went without the meat, and cursed the bread;
And Richard Cory, one calm summer night,
Went home and put a bullet through his head.

Warm-up Activity

After you read the poem, choose the best words to fill in the blanks to complete the sentences.

Richard Cory was a perfect _____ . He was _____ human when he _____ , and he glittered _____ he walked. In short, we thought he was everything to _____ us _____ that we _____ in his place. But one summer _____ , he went _____ and _____ himself and died.

| wish   always   were   gentleman   make   shot   talked   night   home   when |

Questions

1. This poem is told by a first-person plural narrator, "we." What can you guess about the social status of the narrators? Why do "we" envy Richard Cory?

2. What happens in the last part of this poem? Can you imagine why Richard Cory would do such a thing?

Reading Challenge

Alice Walker (1944-) is famous as a novelist; *The Color Purple* (1982) won the National Book Award and the Pulitzer Prize for Fiction and the movie version, directed by Steven Spielberg, was nominated for eleven Academy Awards. Yet she has also published nine books of poetry, beginning in 1968. This poem, "Before I Leave the Stage," appears in her most recent book of poetry, *The World Will Follow Joy: Turning Madness into Flowers* (2014). In one of his plays, William Shakespeare included a speech that begins "All the world's a stage" and compares life to a play. In this context, "leaving the stage" means one is at the end of one's life.

Before I Leave the Stage
Alice Walker

Before I leave the stage
I will sing the only song
I was meant truly to sing.

It is the song
of I AM.
Yes: I am Me
&
You.
WE ARE.

I love Us with every drop
of our blood
every atom of our cells
our waving particles
—undaunted flags of our Being—
neither here nor there.

Questions

1. To "leave the stage" is a figurative expression, that is, it uses metaphor. What does the narrator suggest by using this phrase?

2. What kind of the song does the narrator want to sing? Whose song is it?

Guide 2

Whose voice is speaking inside a poem? The poet's voice, right?

It seems like common sense, doesn't it? A poet feels some emotion and puts his or her emotion into a poem, which is told from the point of view of the poet. It does happen like that sometimes, certainly. Poets are famous for opening their hearts and showing their love or their pain. But do you think that every time a sad love song is written, the writer has a broken heart? Probably not.

Often a poet will create a kind of mask, a kind of imaginary character, who is speaking. This poetic voice or character, sometimes called a "persona," allows the poet to explore many different emotions, not just the ones actually in his or her heart at that moment. For instance, Emily Dickinson, a woman, wrote a poem ("A Narrow Fellow in the Grass") in which she imagined herself to be a young boy who sees a snake in the grass. Her own reaction to a snake in real life might be quite different from the reaction of a young boy, and that is part of the point of the poem.

In the poem "Theme for English B," Langston Hughes uses the voice of a black college student in New York City, but when he wrote the poem he was not attending college and the details of the poem do not fully match his own earlier experiences in college. Walt Whitman, in his long poem *Leaves of Grass*, creates a speaker who calls himself "Walt Whitman," but even though the name is the same, the experiences described often do not match the life Whitman actually lived. In short, the speakers we meet in poems are often quite separate from the writer of the poem, and we should not rush to conclude that a poem only communicates "what the author really wanted to say."

It is probably better for readers to ask, "What character is speaking in this poem?" That way, we can explore the imaginary point of view that is presented. In one of her most famous poems, Emily Dickinson says "I'm nobody. Are you nobody, too?" It is a good question, don't you think? Trying to find the identity of a poem's speaker can sometimes help readers find out their own identities, as well.

Lesson 7
Nature

Word Power

Find the word's best definition and connect it to the word with a line.

demonstrate • • attract
conjure • • describe
haunches • • produce
depict • • buttocks
tempt • • show

underscore • • hatred
distrust • • bad guy
loathing • • emphasize
villain • • suspicion
glide • • move with a smooth continuous motion

swiftly • • wanting
courtesy • • quickly
ashamed • • great respect
deserving • • generosity
veneration • • embarrassed

beclouded • • a jeweled crown
debate • • covered with clouds
complain • • border
diadem • • make a mournful sound
boundary • • consider for a possible course of action

Poem Reading 1

"Fog" may be Carl Sandburg's most famous poem. It has the direct quality of a haiku and it demonstrates Sandburg's ability to conjure images and emotions with simple words.

Fog
Carl Sandburg

The fog comes
on little cat feet.

It sits looking
over harbor and city
on silent haunches
and then moves on.

Warm-up Activity

Read the poem, and then arrange the words to complete the sentences.

The fog _____ on like a cat. It calmly _____ over _____ _____ city, and then _____ somewhere.

goes   and   comes   harbor   looks

Questions

1. Which characteristics of fog does this poem express? Can you fill in the following blank with a suitable word?

   Carl Sandburg uses the image of a cat to express that the fog is _____ .

2. The cat image of the first stanza has an influence on the second stanza. Which words of the second stanza imply the movement of the cat?

Lesson 7

Snakes are powerful symbols in western civilization; in the Bible, Satan was depicted as a serpent that tempts Adam and Eve, resulting in the loss of paradise. This myth underscores the distrust and fear people have of snakes. The hatred is so strong that villains or criminals are sometimes referred to as "snakes."

Snake
Langston Hughes

He glides so swiftly
Back into the grass—
Gives me the courtesy of road
To let me pass,
That I am half ashamed
To seek a stone
To kill him.

Warm-up Activity

Read the poem, and then arrange the words to complete the sentences.

A snake glides so _____ _____ _____ _____ _____ _____ _____ _____ pass, while _____ _____ _____ _____ _____ _____ _____ _____ _____ it.

let grass to the back swiftly me into / kill to am stone I a seeking

Questions

1. What attitude does the narrator have about the snake? How does the snake react when it sees the narrator?

2. Why is the narrator "half ashamed" when he sees the reaction of the snake?

Poem Reading 3

In the West, people often refer to nature as "Mother Nature." By seeing nature as a mother, people perceive that it is deserving of both respect and veneration. In this poem, Dickinson uses a tool of poets called "personification," or giving human characteristics to nonhuman things. Dickinson presents "nature" as if it were a person who can have human tendencies.

Beclouded
Emily Dickinson

The sky is low, the clouds are mean,
A travelling flake of snow
Across a barn or through a rut
Debates if it will go.

A narrow wind complains all day
How some one treated him;
Nature, like us, is sometimes caught
Without her diadem.

Warm-up Activity

After you read the poem, choose the best words to fill in the blanks to complete the sentences.

The winter sky is _____ , and the _____ look cruel. A _____ of snow wonders which way it will _____ . The _____ that runs _____ the _____ space grumbles. Even _____ is sometimes _____ in an _____ condition.

| through   clouds   nature   unhappy   caught   wind   go   low   flake   narrow |

1. Which season does this poem's first stanza depict? Which words in this poem indicate the season?

   ....

   ....

   ....

2. How can nature's unhappy condition be compared to people? What meanings can you find in this comparison?

   ....

   ....

   ....

Reading Challenge

In this poem, Alice Walker refers to the way that boundaries seem to define the substance of what is contained within them. Instead, she suggests, it is the substance that defines the boundaries.

When You See Water
Alice Walker

When you see water in a stream
you say: oh, this is stream
water;
When you see water in the river
you say: oh, this is water
of the river;
When you see ocean
Water
you say: This is the ocean's
water!
But actually water is always
only itself
and does not belong
to any of these containers
though it creates them.
And so it is with you.

Questions

1. How many water images can you find in this poem? How are the images developed?

2. Maybe the water is a metaphor. What does "water" symbolize in this poem?

Lesson 8
Losses in Life

Word Power

Find the word's best definition and connect it to the word with a line.

meticulous • • panic
intent • • catastrophe
fluster • • learn
master • • desire or purpose
disaster • • very careful

realm • • unhappiness
diagnose • • lacking knowledge
depression • • see briefly
glimpse • • land
ignorant • • identify the nature of the medical condition

debris • • turn away from, become unfamiliar
strand • • scattered fragments
anxiety • • uneasiness
estrange • • suffocate
stifle • • shore

pediatrician • • respect
inspire • • real
admire • • a medical practitioner specializing in children
crisp • • stimulate
concrete • • brief

Poem Reading 1

Elizabeth Bishop (1911-1979) was a meticulous crafter of poetry who worked slowly, revising drafts of her poems again and again. As a result, she published only 101 poems in her lifetime. She published her first book in 1946, her second one, *Poems: North & South / A Cold Spring* appeared in 1955 and won the Pulitzer Prize for poetry. "One Art" began as a reflection on losing everyday items: "One might begin by losing one's reading glasses / oh 2 or 3 times a day – or one's favorite pen." Bishop wrote 17 drafts of the poem as she formed it into a villanelle, a 19-line poem that repeats two rhymes. "One Art" is Bishop's most anthologized poem.

One Art
Elizabeth Bishop

The art of losing isn't hard to master;
so many things seem filled with the intent
to be lost that their loss is no disaster.

Lose something every day. Accept the fluster
of lost door keys, the hour badly spent.
The art of losing isn't hard to master.

Then practice losing farther, losing faster:
places, and names, and where it was you meant
to travel. None of these will bring disaster.

I lost my mother's watch. And look! my last, or
next-to-last, of three loved houses went.
The art of losing isn't hard to master.

I lost two cities, lovely ones. And, vaster,
some realms I owned, two rivers, a continent.
I miss them, but it wasn't a disaster.

—Even losing you (the joking voice, a gesture
I love) I shan't have lied. It's evident
the art of losing's not too hard to master
though it may look like (*Write* it!) like disaster.

Warm-up Activity

After you read the poem, choose the best words to fill in the blanks to complete the sentences.

> People always _____ something. Accept the _____ of _____ your everyday things. You can lose door _____ , your mother's _____ , your houses, your _____ . The _____ of losing is not _____ hard _____ master, even when you lose the person _____ you love.

| lands lose losing to keys watch too whom art frustration |

Questions

1. What kind of things have you lost in your past? Exchange some experiences with your classmates.

   _____

   _____

   _____

2. The target of this poem's message is the narrator's beloved. In the last stanza the narrator thinks of the future loss she may suffer, but she presupposes that there will be no need to change her statement, "losing's not too hard to master." Does the narrator really mean it? Why?

   _____

   _____

   _____

Poem Reading 2

Donald Hall (1928 - 2018) attended Harvard, where he met poets such as John Ashbery and Frank O'Hara, before attending Oxford University where he edited the journal *Oxford Poetry*. Hall married poet Jane Kenyon in 1972. Soon they moved to a farm in New Hampshire where they lived and wrote poems. Hall battled cancer, and then his wife was diagnosed with cancer. Hall and Kenyon often wrote poems about living with depression and illness. She died in 1995. Until the end of his life, Hall was still writing poetry that reflected his feelings of loss.

Affirmation
Donald Hall

To grow old is to lose everything.
Aging, everybody knows it.
Even when we are young,
we glimpse it sometimes, and nod our heads
when a grandfather dies.
Then we row for years on the midsummer
pond, ignorant and content. But a marriage,
that began without harm, scatters
into debris on the shore,
and a friend from school drops
cold on a rocky strand.
If a new love carries us
past middle age, our wife will die
at her strongest and most beautiful.
New women come and go. All go.
The pretty lover who announces
that she is temporary
is temporary. The bold woman,
middle-aged against our old age,
sinks under an anxiety she cannot withstand.
Another friend of decades estranges himself
in words that pollute thirty years.
Let us stifle under mud at the pond's edge
and affirm that it is fitting
and delicious to lose everything.

Warm-up Activity

After you read the poem, choose the best words to fill in the blanks to complete the sentences.

When we grow old, we _____ things. In our life, various things happen. We fail in our _____ . We lose our friends. New _____ go away. We lose our longtime friendship easily. But as we grow old and lose precious things, we still affirm that losing _____ can be _____ and intensely interesting.

marriages   lovers   everything   fitting   lose

Questions

1. How many life events do you find in this poem?

2. In the early part of this poem, the narrator states that the young are "ignorant and content." In the last part of this poem the narrator describes losing everything as "fitting and delicious." Why does the narrator evaluate aging this way? When you were young, were you content? What do the old gain when they lose everything?

60

Reading Challenge

William Carlos Williams (1883-1963) earned his living as a pediatrician, that is, a doctor who specializes in the care of babies and children. He published poetry throughout his life, working with and inspiring many other poets who admired Williams's clean, sharp lines and clear images. He met Ezra Pound when they were college students together at the University of Pennsylvania, and learned from Pound the value of brief, image-based writing. One of Williams's most repeated rules of poetry emphasizes the concrete over the imaginary or philosophical: there are "no ideas but in things." In this poem, we can practically taste the plums and taste their coldness.

This Is Just to Say
William Carlos Williams

I have eaten
the plums
that were in
the icebox

and which
you were probably
saving
for breakfast

Forgive me
they were delicious
so sweet
and so cold

Questions

1. What kind of relationship do you imagine between the message writer and the message receiver? Why do you think so?

2. The receiver of this message has lost the delicious experience of the plums. What did the receiver of this message get instead?

Lesson 9
Varieties of Individuality

Word Power

Find the word's or the phrase's best definition and connect them with a line.

cult following • • extremely
reputation • • not central
hard-living • • surviving in difficult conditions
marginal • • common opinion
tremendously • • a small group of strongly devoted fans

glimpse • • tranquility
convey • • sunrise
repose • • tell
dawn • • straight up
upright • • a momentary view

wasted • • being saved
deliberately • • intentionally
unadorned • • extremely unpleasant
obnoxious • • plain
salvation • • misused

inserted • • flourish
humiliated • • added
thrive • • disgraced
restored • • agreement, mutual support
solidarity • • refreshed

Poem Reading 1

Charles Bukowksi (1920 – 1994) published his poems in "little magazines" and small, independent presses for most of his life as he developed a cult following. He cultivated his reputation as a "hard-living" writer – one who drank, gambled, had woman troubles, and struggled to be published as he maintained a marginal existence on the edges of society. His reputation and influence have grown tremendously since his death. This poem gives us a glimpse of his neighborhood where the lives of the people are anything but happy.

and the moon and the stars and the world:
Charles Bukowski

long walks at
night—
that's what's good
for the
soul:
peeking into windows

watching tired
housewives
trying to fight
off
their beer-maddened
husbands.

Warm-up Activity

Read the poem, and then arrange the words to complete the sentences.

Taking _____ _____ _____ _____ _____

_____ _____ the soul because you _____ _____

_____ _____ to _____ _____ _____

_____ with their drunken husbands.

for night at walks long good is / peek windows into can / housewives fighting tired find

Questions

1. Why does the narrator think peeking at the poor American couple's life is good for the soul? Do you think that the speaker intends his words to be taken ironically?

....

....

....

Lesson 9   63

2. Do you want to know other peoples' lives? If so, what might you do instead of peeking into windows at night? Write your own idea and compare it with your classmates' ideas.

....

....

....

Poem Reading 2

One of Bukowski's achievements is his ability to reproduce a simple, commonplace scene in ways that convey a lifestyle. In the context of this poem, one imagines that he has been up all night drinking, and yet he finds a peaceful repose in the morning.

it was just a little while ago
Charles Bukowski

almost dawn
blackbirds on the telephone wire
waiting
as I eat yesterday's
forgotten sandwich
at 6 a.m.
on a quiet Sunday morning.

one shoe in the corner
standing upright
the other laying on its
side.

yes, some lives were made to be
wasted.

Warm-up Activity

Read the poem, and then arrange the words to complete the sentences.

In the Sunday morning I _____ eating the _____ sandwiches even _____ the blackbirds are _____ for them. Some lives were made to _____ wasted.

leftover if am be waiting

Questions

1. Imagine that you are eating yesterday's forgotten sandwich alone on a Sunday morning. How would you feel about your situation?

2. This poem says some lives are made to be wasted. Are you included among such lives, or not? Is it possible that in some ways, wasting time can be a benefit?

Poem Reading 3

This poem, "be kind," is another of Bukowski's poems that seem to be prose. He deliberately wrote in an unadorned, straightforward style to deliver his straightforward message. His hard-edged view of the elderly seems lacking in sympathy, but maybe he is offering a message to readers not to waste their lives. Readers may note an irony because in the previous poem, "it was just a little while ago," the poet seems to accept the fact that he is wasting his own life. And yet, there is also a note of redemption as his life leads to a poem and a perspective. He may also be saying that no one should offer him sympathy in his own old age because he will get the fate he deserves.

be kind
Charles Bukowski

we are always asked
to understand the other person's
viewpoint
no matter how
out-dated
foolish or
obnoxious.

one is asked
to view
their total error
their life-waste
with
kindliness,
especially if they are
aged.

but age is the total of
our doing.
they have aged
badly
because they have
lived
out of focus,
they have refused to
see.

not their fault?

whose fault?
mine?

I am asked to hide
my viewpoint
from them

for fear of their
fear.

age is no crime

but the shame
of a deliberately
wasted
life

among so many
deliberately
wasted
lives

is.

Warm-up Activity

After you read the poem, choose the best words to fill in the blanks to complete the sentences.

We are _____ asked to _____ the other _____ . We are asked to view the other person's error with _____ . But it is a _____ to put the _____ of a _____ wasted _____ among so _____ deliberately _____ lives.

understand life always person wasted shame crime many deliberately kindliness

1. Can you find a suitable word in the poem and fill in the blank in the following sentence?

The shame of a deliberately wasted life among so many deliberately wasted lives is a _____.

2. Why does the narrator mention that there are so many deliberately wasted lives? Is the narrator's life one of them or not? What is the message of the last part of this poem?

....

....

....

Reading Challenge

In this poem, Alice Walker provides her perspective on one of the most famous Bible passages, Jesus's "Sermon on the Mount," which contains a list of blessings referred to as the Beatitudes. In addition to the Beatitude that Walker explores, this list includes, "Blessed are those who mourn, for they will be comforted; Blessed are the meek, for they will inherit the earth," and so on. These Beatitudes have provided encouragement to those who are poor and gentle, suggesting that one day they will find salvation.

Blessed Are the Poor in Spirit
Alice Walker

"Blessed are the poor in spirit (*for theirs is the kingdom of heaven*)."
Did you ever understand this?
If my spirit was poor, how could I enter heaven?
Was I depressed?
Understanding editing,
I see how a comma, removed or inserted
with careful plan,
can change everything.
I was reminded of this
when a poor young man
in Tunisia
desperate to live
and humiliated for trying
set himself ablaze;
I felt uncomfortably warm
as if scalded by his shame.
I do not have to sell vegetables from a cart as he did
or live in narrow rooms too small for spacious thought;
and, at this late date,
I do not worry that someone will
remove every single opportunity
for me to thrive.
Still, I am connected to, inseparable from,
this young man.
Blessed are the poor, in spirit, for theirs is the kingdom of heaven.
Jesus. (Commas restored).

Jesus was as usual talking about solidarity: about how we join with others
and, in spirit, feel the world, and suffering, the same as them.
This is the kingdom of owning the other as self, the self as other—
that transforms grief into
peace and delight.
I, and you, might enter the heaven
of right here
through this door.
In this spirit, knowing we are blessed,
we might remain poor.

Questions

1. Alice Walker's poem is based on a real story of a young man's death in Tunisia. Mohammed Bouazizi, a poor vegetable seller, was regularly a target of the local police's humiliation. On Dec. 17 in 2010, the police harassed him terribly and confiscated his unlicensed vegetable cart. Bouazizi, who felt a strong shame, gave up hope and poured fuel over himself and set himself on fire. Many people became outraged over this incident, and his death became one of the causes of the Tunisian Revolution against the autocratic regime. Alice Walker shares his despair in her spirit. She cannot be completely distinct from him, even though she is now wealthier than he is. Have you had such an experience in your life? Do you feel any compassion for a person who was involved in a shameful humiliation or scandal? Why?

2. What does Alice Walker mean by the last line, that we "might remain poor"? Compare this poem's message with Charles Bukowski's "be kind." Can you find a common message in these two poems?

Guide 3

What can you do with a poem? Describe how it works!

The best way to get to the deeper meanings and emotions of a poem is to go step by step. That means starting with the simple things, the basics. Like the author's name, and the title of the poem. Also, what kind of poem is it? Does the poem have parts? What is the basic situation that is presented in the poem? These are some basic questions that give us a good beginning with any poem.

Here is an example we can start with:

A Noiseless Patient Spider
   by Walt Whitman

A noiseless patient spider,
I mark'd where on a little promontory it stood isolated,
Mark'd how to explore the vacant vast surrounding,
It launch'd forth filament, filament, filament, out of itself,
Ever unreeling them, ever tirelessly speeding them.

And you O my soul where you stand,
Surrounded, detached, in measureless oceans of space,
Ceaselessly musing, venturing, throwing, seeking the spheres to connect them,
Till the bridge you will need be form'd, till the ductile anchor hold,
Till the gossamer thread you fling catch somewhere, O my soul.

Now, step by step:
The author's name is Walt Whitman.
The title of the poem is "A Noiseless Patient Spider."
The poem is a short poem, just 10 lines, which has two parts (or "stanzas").
The first stanza describes a spider making its web.
The second stanza describes the speaker's soul, searching for a place in the universe.

We can take these basic notes about the poem and combine them into a summary and comment on the poem, like this:

Walt Whitman's short poem, "A Noiseless Patient Spider," has only two stanzas. The first part shows a spider building its web by leaping into space again and again. In the second part, the speaker talks directly to his soul, which is endlessly trying to find a place in the universe. The surprising comparison of a person's soul to a spider hints about the constant search for meaning in life.

This kind of summary and comment is the written foundation for more advanced study of poems—and in fact it can be used when we study other kinds of writing, such as stories or novels or films. Simple, right? And this kind of short paragraph of 4-6 sentences can be a template for the first version of the essays you write about poetry, fiction, and film.

If we use the template to comment on Emily Dickinson's poem about making a prairie, it might look like this:

Emily Dickinson's short poem "To Make a Prairie" has only five lines, and just two sentences. The first sentence gives a simple "recipe" for creating a prairie. Only three ingredients are needed: a clover, a bee, and "revery," or imagination. The second sentence, which is a surprising conclusion, suggests that all three ingredients are not necessary, in fact. The main idea presented at the end is that imagination alone is powerful enough to create grand natural scenes that we can enjoy.

The specific content will be different in each case, of course, but the general template gives us a useful pattern for writing that we can quickly master. Naturally, we can change the sentence patterns we use, so our comments have some variety, but the order of the content can be the same in almost every case. Try it for yourself on one of the poems in this book!

Lesson 9

Lesson 10
Loneliness

Word Power

Find the word's or the phrase's best definition and connect them with a line.

reputation • • mainly
perplex • • praise enthusiastically
overtime • • an evaluation by the public
primarily • • confuse
extol • • in the meanwhile

encompass • • with a burning desire
intimate • • informal
longingly • • include
flit by each other • • familiar
folksy • • pass by each other

acquainted with • • street
outwalked • • patrolman
lane • • reluctant
watchman • • walked further than
unwilling • • familiar with

unearthly • • announce
luminary • • savage
proclaim • • unnaturally
bestial • • sit on one's heels
squat • • bright

Poem Reading 1

According to the *Poetry Foundation*, Walt Whitman (1819-1892) is "America's world poet—a latter-day successor to Homer, Virgil, Dante, and Shakespeare." His reputation rests on his book *Leaves of Grass* that he first published in 1855 and revised for the rest of his life. When these poems appeared, readers were perplexed by their style and upset by their frankness. Over time, his reputation has grown. Whitman wrote primarily about America and its citizens, extolling his profound belief in the future of democracy. His poems encompass vast stretches of history and land, yet they are also immediately appealing to readers in personal and even intimate ways. He began his writing career as a newspaper journalist, an occupation that aided him in developing his sense of audience and in making a direct address to the reader, as he does in this poem.

To a Stranger
Walt Whitman

Passing stranger! you do not know how longingly I look upon you,
You must be he I was seeking, or she I was seeking, (it comes to me as of a dream,)
I have somewhere surely lived a life of joy with you,
All is recall'd as we flit by each other, fluid, affectionate, chaste, matured,
You grew up with me, were a boy with me or a girl with me,
I ate with you and slept with you, your body has become not yours only nor left my body mine only,
You give me the pleasure of your eyes, face, flesh, as we pass, you take of my beard, breast, hands, in return,
I am not to speak to you, I am to think of you when I sit alone or wake at night alone,
I am to wait, I do not doubt I am to meet you again,
I am to see to it that I do not lose you.

＊see to it that〜：〜するよう取り計らう

Warm-up Activity

After you read the poem, choose the best words to fill in the blanks to complete the sentences.

> I pass you, stranger, yet I feel that we have known each _____ before. Although I do not _____ to you, I feel that we are very close and that we will stay connected. I think of you when I sit alone or wake at _____ alone. I do not _____ I am to meet you _____ .

night speak other again doubt

Lesson 10

Questions

1. In his inner voice, the narrator calls to a stranger and believes that he has "somewhere surely lived a life of joy" with the stranger. In what ways might the narrator have shared the joy of life with the stranger?

2. Why does the narrator believe that he will meet the stranger again in the future? How does this poem suggest the loneliness of the narrator, in spite of the positive tone of this poem?

Poem Reading 2

Robert Frost (1874-1963) was, during his lifetime, one of America's favorite poets. For much of the twentieth century, his poems represented what many readers thought of when they imagined what poetry ought to be like. He wrote poems in traditional forms that usually included rhyme and concluded with a sense of resolution. Although his poems seemed to many readers to impart a kind of easy-going, folksy wisdom, he warned readers not to take him too lightly. Poems like "Acquainted with the Night" provide a form that seems to console, while the core message warns of the terrors beyond human understanding.

＊rhyme: 脚韻

Acquainted with the Night
Robert Frost

I have been one acquainted with the night.
I have walked out in rain—and back in rain.
I have outwalked the furthest city light.

I have looked down the saddest city lane.
I have passed by the watchman on his beat
And dropped my eyes, unwilling to explain.

I have stood still and stopped the sound of feet
When far away an interrupted cry
Came over houses from another street,

But not to call me back or say good-bye;
And further still at an unearthly height,
One luminary clock against the sky

Proclaimed the time was neither wrong nor right
I have been one acquainted with the night.

Warm-up Activity

After you read the poem, choose the best words to fill in the blanks to complete the sentences.

I know the _____ very well. I have walked to the _____ part of the city, or looked _____ the saddest city _____ . I have _____ dark streets and passed by the _____ . I have _____ still when I heard a distant _____ . I have watched the _____ as if it were a _____ that can never be wrong — or right.

furthest   walked   night   moon   stood   watchman   down   clock   lane   cry

Questions

1. From the third to the final stanza, the narrator takes another long walk. What does he hear in the middle of the walk? How does he react to it?

2. "One luminary clock against the sky" means the moon at night. Is this moon friendly to the narrator or not? Why do you think so?

Lesson 10   73

Reading Challenge

"In the Desert" is another of Stephen Crane's "lines," that is, one of the modern-style verses he crafted in the language of everyday speech that conveys a dark message. This message may be one that warns us of spending too much of our time casting bad will at others, or at ourselves.

In the Desert
Stephen Crane

In the desert
I saw a creature, naked, bestial,
Who, squatting upon the ground,
Held his heart in his hands,
And ate of it.
I said: "Is it good, friend?"
"It is bitter—bitter," he answered;
"But I like it
Because it is bitter,
And because it is my heart."

Questions

1. The narrator calls the creature his "friend." Why does the narrator use this term?

2. Compare this poem with Robert Frost's "Acquainted with the Night." What kinds of things are the narrators acquainted with in these two poems?

Lesson 11
Poets and Poetry (1)

W o r d   P o w e r

Find the word's or the phrase's best definition and connect them with a line.

seclusion • • shyness
reticence • • fellow citizens
obscurity • • peculiarity
idiosyncrasy • • anonymity
countrymen • • isolation

characteristic • • judging character from facial characteristics
first-person speaker • • feature
En-Masse • • the goddess of poetic inspiration
physiognomy • • narrator who refers to himself as "I"
Muse • • all together

immense • • continuing
affluent • • extremely large
accessible • • distress
enduring • • understandable
afflict • • rich

allude to • • principally
predominantly • • suggest
juniper • • a great distress
shagged • • an evergreen tree
misery • • covered

Poem Reading 1

Emily Dickinson (1830-1866) is known for living a quiet private life of seclusion in Amherst, Massachusetts. Nonetheless, she read widely and exchanged many letters. Her desire for privacy may have been largely responsible for her lack of fame during her lifetime; she shared poems in her letters to her friends but no one realized the extent of her genius. After her death, her family found nearly 1,800 poems, and her first collection of poems, in severely edited forms, was published four years later. The versions of poems included here follow the later publications that sought to restore the odd characteristics of her handwritten versions. Notice the unusual capitalizations and dashes.

This is my letter to the World
Emily Dickinson

This is my letter to the World
That never wrote to Me —
The simple News that Nature told —
With tender Majesty

Her Message is committed
To Hands I cannot see —
For love of Her — Sweet — countrymen —
Judge tenderly — of Me

Warm-up Activity

Read the poem, and then arrange the words to complete the sentences.

My poem _____ _____ _____ _____ _____
world. I _____ _____ _____ _____ _____
my poem kindly and not blame me.

to   letter   the   my   is   /   to   readers   understand   my   ask

76

uestions

1. Whose message does the poem's letter bring? Is the narrator only Emily Dickinson?

2. Emily Dickinson refers to her own poem as a "letter" to the world, which has never written to her. Compare this attitude with Walt Whitman's "To a Stranger." Why do these two authors send their messages to unknown persons? Do they share the same purpose? If not, what are the differences in their purposes?

Poem Reading 2

One characteristic of Whitman's poetry is his attempt to find equality in all aspects of humanity. This democratic sense put him ahead of many of his countrymen in the middle of the 19th century. Whitman's first person speaker in *Leaves of Grass* is not limited to "Walt," as he identifies himself in this poem, but expands to include all Americans past, present, and future.

One's-Self I Sing
Walt Whitman

One's-Self I sing, a simple separate person,
Yet utter the word Democratic, the word En-Masse.

Of physiology from top to toe I sing,
Not physiognomy alone nor brain alone is worthy for the Muse, I say the Form complete is worthier far,
The Female equally with the Male I sing.

Of Life immense in passion, pulse, and power,
Cheerful, for freest action form'd under the laws divine,
The Modern Man I sing.

Warm-up Activity

After you read the poem, choose the best words to fill in the blanks to complete the sentences.

Singing of the _____ is one of my most important themes. I _____ every element of the body and _____ of men and _____ . I sing of _____ man's human life that is great in passion, _____ , and power, and is cheerful _____ its _____ action _____ under God's _____ laws.

| mind | in | women | sing | modern | divine | Self | pulse | formed | freest |

Questions

1. To whom is Walt Whitman singing this poem? Is he singing this poem only for himself?

2. Do you feel Walt Whitman's words are democratic? Why or why not?

Poem Reading 3

"What is the blues?" is an enduring question, usually asked by people who are outside the blues tradition. Langston Hughes makes an attempt to answer this question in a manner that is easily accessible to his readers. The humorous surface of the poem addresses the kind of troubles that may afflict a child, but Hughes manages to allude to issues of poverty and hunger, as well as the distance between the affluent and the poor.

The Blues
Langston Hughes

When the shoe strings break
On *both* your shoes
And you're in a hurry —
That's the blues.

When you go to buy a candy bar
And you've lost the dime you had —
Slipped through a hole in your pocket somewhere —
That's the blues, too, *and bad!*

Warm-up Activity

After you read the poem, choose the best words to fill in the blanks to complete the sentences.

> You feel the _____ when you are in a _____ but the shoestrings _____ on both of your _____. Or you feel the blues when you _____ to buy a _____ bar and you find that you have lost the _____ through a _____ in your _____. Singing about _____ things in a human way is the blues.

hurry bad blues candy go shoes hole dime break pocket

Questions

1. The blues is a genre of music that possesses a mournful and haunting character, originating among the African Americans. This poem makes some additional points about the word. What aspects of life are added to the blues in this poem?

Lesson 11   79

2. Langston Hughes suggests that the blues are made for whom?

Reading Challenge

Wallace Stevens (1879-1955) was a lawyer who worked for a large insurance company, where he rose to the position of vice president. During this career, he wrote the poems that led to his winning the Pulitzer Prize for poetry in 1955. Unlike William Carlos Williams, who believed there were "no ideas but in things," Stevens was predominantly a poet of ideas. "The Snow Man" consists of one sentence that leads the reader to contemplate the related concepts of existence and nothingness.

The Snow Man
Wallace Stevens

One must have a mind of winter
To regard the frost and the boughs
Of the pine-trees crusted with snow;

And have been cold a long time
To behold the junipers shagged with ice,
The spruces rough in the distant glitter

Of the January sun; and not to think
Of any misery in the sound of the wind,
In the sound of a few leaves,

Which is the sound of the land
Full of the same wind
That is blowing in the same bare place

For the listener, who listens in the snow,
And, nothing himself, beholds
Nothing that is not there and the nothing that is.

＊spruce=スプルースあるいはトウヒ。マツ科の常緑高木。

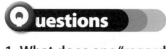

1. What does one "regard" and "behold" in the first and second part of this poem?

2. If a person "has a mind of winter," and "is not to think of any misery," what is the state of their mind? Is that mental state the same as just trying to escape?

Lesson 12
Poets and Poetry (2)

Word Power

Find the word's or the phrase's best definition and connect them with a line.

isolation • • remaining alone
vastness • • premier
foremost • • a huge space
acquaintance • • the ability to live forever
immortality • • a person one knows slightly

corporeal • • passionately
with ease • • bodily
absorb • • a unit of pronunciation
syllable • • soak up
fervently • • smoothly

defer • • unreal
a household name • • contradiction
surreal • • postpone
phrasing • • a famous person
paradox • • putting into words

oxymoron • • provoke humorously
fidget • • apparently inconsistent terms（撞着語法）
chatter • • choose
tease • • talk in a way that is not serious
adopt • • move restlessly

Poem Reading 1

Emily Dickinson spent most of her life in isolation, living upstairs in her family home, where she explored the universe in her imagination. In "The Brain," she points out the vastness of the human brain, that is, a person's ability to know and to imagine. Unlike Whitman, who equally valued both mind and body, Dickinson seemed to place the importance of the mind foremost. In a letter to a trusted literary acquaintance, she wrote, "A letter always feels to me like immortality because it is the mind alone without corporeal friend."

The Brain
Emily Dickinson

The brain is wider than the sky,
   For, put them side by side,
The one the other will include
   With ease, and you beside.

The brain is deeper than the sea,
   For, hold them, blue to blue,
The one the other will absorb,
   As sponges, buckets do.

The brain is just the weight of God,
   For, lift them, pound for pound,
And they will differ, if they do,
   As syllable from sound.

Warm-up Activity

Read the poem, and then arrange the words to complete the sentences.

> The brain is large and it can _____ the whole world. Like sponges _____ up the buckets of _____, the brain absorbs the seawater. The brain's words are _____ _____ same as God's sounds.

soak contain the water much

Lesson 12

Questions

1. In this poem, Emily Dickinson declares the brain is "wider than the sky" and "deeper than the sea." How could this possibly be true?

2. Compare this poem to Emily Dickinson's "This is my letter to the World." Do you think these two poems say something about the power and value of a single person's mental life?

Poem Reading 2

Langston Hughes believed fervently in the importance of dreams. For example, in a poem simply titled "Dreams," he wrote "if dreams die / Life is a broken-winged bird / That cannot fly." One of his most famous poems is "Harlem," in which he asks, "What happens to a dream deferred? / Does it dry up / like a raisin in the sun?"

The Dream Keeper
Langston Hughes

Bring me all of your dreams,
You dreamers,
Bring me all your
Heart melodies
That I may wrap them
In a blue cloud-cloth
Away from the too-rough fingers
Of the world.

Warm-up Activity

Read the poem, and then choose the best words to complete the sentences.

> Bring me your private dreams. I _____ _____ _____
> _____ dreams carefully. I _____ _____ _____
> _____ _____ _____ away place.

your will up wrap / in far a will them store

Questions

1. Why does the poet wrap up the people's dreams and melodies? How does the poet imagine the world?

   _____

   _____

   _____

2. According to this poem, in what way is the poet related to the people? What is the poet producing?

   _____

   _____

   _____

Reading Challenge

John Ashbery (1927-2017) has won the Pulitzer Prize, the National Book Award, and the National Book Critics Circle Award, yet he has never become a household name. That may be because his poems are considered to be "difficult," or challenging to readers, due in part to their surreal images and unique phrasing. In this poem, Ashbery seems to be letting his readers know how they might approach his work, or any poem.

Paradoxes and Oxymorons
John Ashbery

This poem is concerned with language on a very plain level.
Look at it talking to you. You look out a window
Or pretend to fidget. You have it but you don't have it.
You miss it, it misses you. You miss each other.

The poem is sad because it wants to be yours, and cannot be.
What's a plain level? It is that and other things,
Bringing a system of them into play. Play?
Well, actually, yes, but I consider play to be

A deeper outside thing, a dreamed role-pattern,
As in the division of grace these long August days
Without proof. Open-ended. And before you know it
It gets lost in the steam and chatter of typewriters.

It has been played once more. I think you exist only
To tease me into doing it, on your level, and then you aren't there
Or have adopted a different attitude. And the poem
Has set me softly down beside you. The poem is you.

Questions

1. Compare this song with Langston Hughes' "The Dream Keeper." In Langston Hughes' "The Dream Keeper," the relationship between the dream keeper and people's dreams and melodies is simpler. Why does John Ashbery feel that it is difficult to catch a poem's meaning?

2. The narrator of this poem seems to communicate with "you" through the poem. How is this communication completed?

Guide 4

What are symbols, and what are they useful for?

Whenever people talk about poems—or any other kind of literature, actually—they are probably going to mention symbols, aren't they? But it can seem so mysterious, all this talk about symbols. Why do we have to hide the meanings behind symbols? Wouldn't it be better to say what we mean? What exactly is a symbol, anyway?

Symbols do not have to seem so mysterious, actually. Almost certainly you have used symbols, and probably many times today. Think about it this way. A symbol is a thing. Maybe some object or some image. This thing acts like a substitute or replacement for an idea or an emotion.

Take emojis, for instance. If you input an emoji that looks like a red heart, that is an image; it is a thing. However, everyone knows that it has a meaning, and the meaning is "love." An object is used to communicate meanings and emotions indirectly. If we are talking about literature, we can say the same thing; using a symbol is a way to communicate themes. We can change the symbol a bit sometimes, too. An emoji of a face with red hearts for eyes probably means "I feel love whenever I see you." Obviously, symbols are everywhere, then, and not just emojis. General symbols like these within a culture are sometimes called cultural symbols.

Symbols in literature are a bit more complicated and interesting, however. A poet can create new connections between some object and a meaning. The context of the symbol and theme help us to discover the new connections, and that is part of the creative pleasure of poetry.

Let's take the example of Whitman's poem, "The Noiseless, Patient Spider." Probably, most readers do not have any symbolic understanding of spiders. They are just spiders. Or maybe some people think they are frightening or creepy. But Whitman creates a new connection. In the first part of his poem he describes the spider making its world, its "web," out of its self. Then, in the second part, he says indirectly: that is just like my soul, which is creating a new world out of its own self. In this way, Whitman gives us a chance to discover new images and meanings: I am endlessly creating my own place in the universe, just as a spider endlessly creates its own world.

In fact, there is some cultural symbolism connected to spiders. In some parts of the US, people think you will die if a spider "writes" your name in its web. In some parts of Japan, finding a spiderweb in the house means an old friend will come to visit. These are cultural symbols, and will change only slowly and gradually. But Whitman's spider symbol was created just for the purposes of this one poem, and the symbolic poem gives readers a chance to uncover various new meanings for themselves.

Spiders may seem like a weird example of a symbol, but in fact the spider appears fairly often in literature. Spider Man is a famous example from popular comics and movie culture, and in traditional Japanese drama we can find the famous character of the Tsuchigumo. Emily Dickinson has given us at least two poems about spiders: "The Spider as an Artist" and "The Spider Holds a Silver Ball." Neither of those poems has the same symbolic meanings we find in Whitman's poem; both of her poems reveal new ideas and emotions with the symbol of the spider.

Literary symbols do something very creative and important: they build new networks of ideas and emotions, and allow us to expand our ways of thinking about ourselves and the world.

Lesson 12

Lesson 13
Settings of Love and Life

Word Power

Find the word's best definition and connect it to the word with a line.

implore • • a group of lines in a poem
stanza • • request
maiden • • destiny
fate • • red
ruddy • • a young unmarried woman

lingered • • ring of light
splendor • • praise
halo • • waited
worship • • considered
deemed • • magnificence

subtle • • growled
infuse • • delicate
whisper • • clattered
snarled • • fill
rattled • • speak softly

scented • • short breath
rueful • • perfumed
ether • • heartbeat
puff • • regretful
pulse • • gas for anesthesia（麻酔）

Poem Reading 1

Ella Wheeler Wilcox (1850-1919) was a remarkably positive poet who implored her readers to see the best in life. Her poems typically consist of traditional stanza forms and simple rhymes. One of her sentiments from her poem "Solitude" is particularly well known: "Laugh, and the world laughs with you; / Weep, and you weep alone.""Long Ago" demonstrates that Wilcox could be rueful as well.

Long Ago
Ella Wheeler Wilcox

I loved a maiden, long ago,
    She held within her hand my fate;
And in the ruddy sunset glow
    We lingered at the garden gate.

The splendor of the western skies
    Lay in a halo on her hair.
I gazed with worship in her eyes,
    And deemed her true and knew her fair.

"Good night," I said, and turned away;
    She held me with her subtle smile.
I saw her red lips whisper "stay,"
    And so I lingered yet awhile.

"I love you, love you, sweet!" I said,
    She laughed, and whispered, "I love you."
I kissed her small mouth, ripe and red,
    And knew her fair, and deemed her true.

'Twas very, very long ago,
    And I was young, and so was she;
My faith as love was strong, for oh!
    The maid was all the world to me.

But as the sunset died away
    And left the heavens cold and blue,
So died my dream of love one day.
    The maid was only fair, *not* true.

Warm-up Activity

After you read the poem, choose the best words to fill in the blanks to complete the sentences.

A long time ago I loved a woman. I met her at the _____ gate in the ruddy _____ time. I _____ with _____ in her eyes, and considered that she is my _____ love. She asked me to stay longer with her _____ and I _____ with her at the garden gate for a while. I was _____ , and so _____ she. She was _____ the world to me. But finally she turned out to be unfaithful to me.

gazed   garden   was   smile   true   worship   young   lingered   sunset   all

Questions

1. This is a love poem. What kind of power relationship can you find in this poem between the narrator and the maiden? Which has love's advantages?

2. What is the narrator's "dream of love"? Is it possible to consider that a girl can be "all the world" to a man? What is wrong with the narrator's youthful thinking?

Poem Reading 2

Robert Frost wrote many narrative poems in "blank verse," or unrhymed lines of iambic pentameter. That is, each line has five stressed syllables. Blank verse is one of the most common forms of poetry for long narrative poems. John Milton's book-length poem "Paradise Lost" and most of William Shakespeare's plays are written in blank verse. Frost infused his lines with particularly American expressions and figures of speech.

"Out, Out—"
Robert Frost

The buzz-saw snarled and rattled in the yard
And made dust and dropped stove-length sticks of wood,
Sweet-scented stuff when the breeze drew across it.
And from there those that lifted eyes could count
Five mountain ranges one behind the other
Under the sunset far into Vermont.
And the saw snarled and rattled, snarled and rattled,
As it ran light, or had to bear a load.
And nothing happened: day was all but done.
Call it a day, I wish they might have said
To please the boy by giving him the half hour
That a boy counts so much when saved from work.
His sister stood beside them in her apron
To tell them "Supper." At the word, the saw,
As if to prove saws knew what supper meant,
Leaped out at the boy's hand, or seemed to leap—
He must have given the hand. However it was,
Neither refused the meeting. But the hand!
The boy's first outcry was a rueful laugh,
As he swung toward them holding up the hand
Half in appeal, but half as if to keep
The life from spilling. Then the boy saw all—
Since he was old enough to know, big boy
Doing a man's work, though a child at heart—
He saw all spoiled. "Don't let him cut my hand off—
The doctor, when he comes. Don't let him, sister!"
So. But the hand was gone already.
The doctor put him in the dark of ether.
He lay and puffed his lips out with his breath.
And then—the watcher at his pulse took fright.
No one believed. They listened at his heart.
Little—less—nothing!—and that ended it.
No more to build on there. And they, since they
Were not the one dead, turned to their affairs.

Warm-up Activity

Read the poem, and then arrange the words to complete the sentences.

A boy is helping with the timber work in the mountainside. But when the boy's _____ _____ beside them in her apron to tell them it was time for supper, the buzz-saw leaped out at the boy's hand and cut it, as _____ to _____ it _____ what supper meant. The hand has gone. The doctor attempted to save him, but he suddenly died. The people went back to work.

stood   sister   prove   knew   if

Questions

1. What happened to the boy at the end of the poem? How did the other people react to the boy's accident?

   ....
   ....
   ....

2. What kind of shared sentiment can you find in Ella Wheeler Wilcox's "Long Ago" and Robert Frost's "Out, Out—"? How do these two poems treat the unfaithful maiden and the dead boy?

   ....
   ....
   ....

Lesson 14

Imagination

Word Power

Find the word's or the phrase's best definition and connect them with a line.

perceive • • superficial
apparent • • recognize
tranquility • • sleepless
restless • • rouse from sleep
awaken • • peace; calmness

roaming • • not reactive to
uneasily • • wandering
growling • • nervously
keys • • making a snarling sound
unresponsive to • • islands

coarse-fibred (coarse-fibered) • • heap
limp • • rough, hairy
fistfuls • • in lines
in rows • • soft
pile • • handfuls

uninjured • • avenue
barely • • humorously
boulevard • • not damaged
wittily • • confused
disconcerted • • scarcely

Poem Reading 1

Langston Hughes, who had worked as a seaman, perceives trouble even in apparent calmness. As a black man writing during the Jim Crow era in the United States, Hughes knew that he should never trust a surface appearance of peace or tranquility.

*Jim Crow=the former practice of segregating black people in the US

Sea Calm
Langston Hughes

How still,
How strangely still
The water is today.
It is not good
For water
To be so still that way.

Warm-up Activity

Read the poem, and then arrange the words to complete the sentences.

> The water is calm. It _____ _____ _____ _____ _____ _____ _____ _____ _____ such a way.

| to still is so for be water the unnatural in |

Questions

1. Except for the title, the word "sea" does not appear in this poem. Why does the narrator choose not to use the word "sea" in the body of this poem?

_____

_____

_____

94

2. Who believes that still water is "not good" in this poem? Can we imagine who this narrator might be?

_____

_____

_____

Poem Reading 2

When this poem by Elizabeth Bishop was first published in 1946, her original title was "Little Exercise at 4 A.M.," and one imagines a restless person in the night, awakened perhaps by the unseen thunderstorm outside. The word "exercise" here refers to "practice," as a student learning to play piano might practice an exercise from a lesson book. In this poem, Bishop asks her readers to exercise their imaginations in order to "see" what is happening outside.

Little Exercise
Elizabeth Bishop

Think of the storm roaming the sky uneasily
like a dog looking for a place to sleep in,
listen to it growling.

Think how they must look now, the mangrove keys
lying out there unresponsive to the lightning
in dark, coarse-fibred families,

where occasionally a heron may undo his head,
shake up his feathers, make an uncertain comment
when the surrounding water shines.

Think of the boulevard and the little palm trees
all stuck in rows, suddenly revealed
as fistfuls of limp fish-skeletons.

It is raining there. The boulevard
and its broken sidewalks with weeds in every crack
are relieved to be wet, the sea to be freshened.

Now the storm goes away again in a series
of small, badly lit battle-scenes,
each in "Another part of the field."

Think of someone sleeping in the bottom of a row-boat
tied to a mangrove root or the pile of a bridge;
think of him as uninjured, barely disturbed.

Warm-up Activity

After you read the poem, choose the best words to fill in the blanks to complete the sentences.

This is a little exercise of imagination. Think of the storm _____ the sky _____ . Think of the _____ islands that are lying _____ there under the _____ in the dark storm. Think of how the bird _____ up its _____ , and makes a noisy cry. Think of the wet _____ and the storm-beaten little _____ trees. Now the storm goes away. Think of someone who has not been disturbed by the storm, sleeping in the _____ of the boat.

uneasily lightning bottom feathers boulevard out shakes mangrove roaming palm

Questions

1. What kinds of dramas does this narrator require readers to imagine?

2. The last stanza begins with a possibly dangerous scene, but then assures the reader that everything is OK. Do you really think so? What is the overall effect of the poem?

Reading Challenge

Ralph Waldo Emerson (1803-1882) was a prominent 19th century philosopher, lecturer, poet, and editor. His lectures and publications helped define American romanticism and created a movement called Transcendentalism. In "Water," Emerson may have found an element that is more powerful, and longer lasting, than civilization.

Water
Ralph Waldo Emerson

The water understands
Civilization well;
It wets my foot, but prettily,
It chills my life, but wittily,
It is not disconcerted,
It is not broken-hearted:
Well used, it decketh joy,
Adorneth, doubleth joy:
Ill used, it will destroy,
In perfect time and measure
With a face of golden pleasure
Elegantly destroy.

*decketh=decks   * adorneth=adorns   * doubleth=doubles

Questions

1. In what ways do we control water? Do you think that we can control water completely?

2. What kind of disaster might result when we "ill use" water – that is, when we use water badly?

Lesson 14   97

Lesson 15
America

Word Power

Find the word's or the phrase's best definition and connect them with a line.

hymns	you
a theological student	religious songs
thee	as a result
consequently	the words of a poem or song
lyric	a student whose specialty is God and religion
anthem	blissful happiness
prominently	a patriotic song
rapture	particularly
prolong	sympathetic
harmonious	extend
enhance	happy; cheerful
diverse	increase; improve
carols	various
blithe	strong; healthy
robust	songs
sweltering	elevate
vicious	cut
exalt	hot
hew	disagreement
discord	brutal

Poem Reading 1

Samuel Francis Smith (1808-1895) was a Baptist minister who wrote more than 150 hymns, or religious songs of praise. While a theological student in Germany, Smith composed "My Country 'Tis of Thee," which has been sung by American school children since 1832. According to the *Songwriters Hall of Fame*, Smith may have heard German schoolchildren singing a hymn to begin their school day, and he desired to have a similar song for American school children. Consequently, he wrote the lyrics and set them to the melody of the British anthem, "God Save the King." In 1963, Martin Luther King, Jr. referred to Smith's nationally known song when he prominently featured the phrase "Let freedom ring" in his "I Have a Dream" speech.

My Country, 'Tis of Thee
Samuel Francis Smith

My country, 'tis of thee,
Sweet land of liberty,
  Of thee I sing;
Land where my fathers died,
Land of the pilgrim's pride,
From every mountain side
  Let Freedom ring!

My native country thee,
Land of the noble free,
  Thy name I love.
I love thy rocks and rills,
Thy woods and templed hills
My heart with rapture thrills
  Like that above.

Let music swell the breeze
And ring from all the trees,
  Sweet freedom's song,
Let mortal tongues awake;
Let all that breathes partake:
Let rocks their silence break,
  The sound prolong.
Our father's God to thee.
Author of liberty,
  To thee we sing:

Long may our land be bright
With freedom's holy light;
Protect us by thy might,
  Great God, our King!

---

*'tis =it is

*pilgrim's pride= The pride inherited from a group of English Puritans fleeing religious persecution who sailed in the Mayflower and founded the colony of Plymouth, Massachusetts, in 1620.

Warm-up Activity

After you read the poem, choose the best words to fill in the blanks to complete the sentences.

> I sing of my country America, the sweet _____ of liberty. Let _____ ring from every mountain side. You're my _____ country, land of the _____ free. I love your _____ . I love my country's rocks, rills, _____ and hills. Let music _____ the breeze and _____ from all the trees. We sing to our God, the _____ of liberty. We hope our land will be _____ with freedom's holy light.

woods noble bright land native author swell name freedom ring

Questions

1. These are the lyrics of a patriotic song. How does this song express the American spirit? What kind of land is it?

2. The narrator calls for all things to participate in the singing of the song; even the rocks should sing. How do you interpret it?

Poem Reading 2

No American poet is more patriotic than Walt Whitman, and above all he valued the individual people of the nation. He wrote in his preface to *Leaves of Grass* (1855), "The United States themselves are essentially the greatest poem." He may have meant that the voices of the common and diverse American people, even as they differ on many issues, come together to form a harmonious nation. He composed his verses in common vocabulary that he enhanced with his measured phrasing and tone so that anyone, including the everyday people he wrote about, could understand and be inspired by them.

I Hear America Singing
Walt Whitman

I hear America singing, the varied carols I hear,
Those of mechanics, each one singing his as it should be blithe and strong,
The carpenter singing his as he measures his plank or beam,
The mason singing his as he makes ready for work, or leaves off work,
The boatman singing what belongs to him in his boat, the deckhand singing on the steamboat deck,
The shoemaker singing as he sits on his bench, the hatter singing as he stands,
The wood-cutter's song, the ploughboy's on his way in the morning, or at noon intermission or at sundown,
The delicious singing of the mother, or of the young wife at work, or of the girl sewing or washing,
Each singing what belongs to him or her and to none else,
The day what belongs to the day — at night the party of young fellows, robust, friendly,
Singing with open mouths their strong melodious songs.

＊ploughboy=plowboy; country boy

Warm-up Activity

After you read the poem, choose the best words to fill in the blanks to complete the sentences.

I hear America singing, the varied songs I hear, the songs of _____, the _____, the _____, the _____, the deckhand, the _____, the hatter, the _____, the _____, the _____, the young _____, the _____. Each of them is singing about what belongs to him or her. They are singing with open mouths their strong melodious songs.

wife ploughboy shoemaker carpenter wood-cutter mechanics mother girl mason boatman

Lesson 15   101

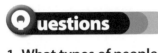

Questions

1. What types of people appear in this poem?

2. Why do you think Walt Whitman did not mention the teacher, the politician, or the newspaperman?

Reading Challenge

Martin Luther King, Jr. (1929-1968) was a Baptist minister and civil rights leader who came to prominence as a key figure in the civil rights movement. He tirelessly championed the cause of racial equality in the United States while insisting that his followers use only non-violent methods of protest. In 1963, he spoke from the steps of the Lincoln Memorial in Washington D.C before a crowd of 250,000 people. His speech became known by the title "I Have a Dream." The following year, King was awarded the Nobel Peace Prize. He was assassinated in 1968. His speech lives on as one of the most inspiring speeches ever recorded, and millions of Americans have committed at least a portion of this speech to memory.

I Have a Dream
Martin Luther King Jr.

I have a dream that one day on the red hills of Georgia, the sons of former slaves and the sons of former slave owners will be able to sit down together at the table of brotherhood.

I have a dream that one day even the state of Mississippi, a state sweltering with the heat of injustice, sweltering with the heat of oppression, will be transformed into an oasis of freedom and justice.

I have a dream that my four little children will one day live in a nation where they will not be judged by the color of their skin but by the content of their character. I have a dream today.

I have a dream that one day down in Alabama, with its vicious racists, with its governor having his lips dripping with the words of "interposition" and "nullification," one day right there in Alabama little black boys and black girls will be able to join hands with little white boys and white girls as sisters and brothers. I have a dream today.

I have a dream that one day every valley shall be exalted, and every hill and mountain shall be made low; the rough places will be made plain, and the crooked places will be made straight; and the glory of the Lord shall be revealed, and all flesh shall see it together.

This is our hope. This is the faith that I go back to the South with. With this faith we will be able to hew out of the mountain of despair a stone of hope. With this faith we will be able to transform the jangling discords of our nation into a beautiful symphony of brotherhood. With this faith we will be able to work together, to pray together, to struggle together, to go to jail together, to stand up for freedom together, knowing that we will be free one day. This will be the day, this will be the day when all of God's children will be able to sing with new meaning:

> My country, 'tis of thee, sweet land of liberty, of thee I sing.
> Land where my fathers died, land of the pilgrims' pride,
> From every mountainside, let freedom ring!

And if America is to be a great nation, this must become true.
And so let freedom ring from the prodigious hilltops of New Hampshire.
Let freedom ring from the mighty mountains of New York.
Let freedom ring from the heightening Alleghenies of Pennsylvania.
Let freedom ring from the snowcapped Rockies of Colorado.
Let freedom ring from the curvaceous slopes of California.
But not only that: Let freedom ring from Stone Mountain of Georgia.
Let freedom ring from Lookout Mountain of Tennessee.
Let freedom ring from every hill and molehill of Mississippi. From every mountainside,
    let freedom ring.

And when this happens, when we allow freedom [to] ring, when we let it ring from every village and every hamlet, from every state and every city, we will be able to speed up that day when all of God's children, black men and white men, Jews and Gentiles, Protestants and Catholics, will be able to join hands and sing in the words of the old Negro spiritual:

> Free at last! Free at last!
> Thank God Almighty, we are free at last!

---

*all flesh=all human beings

Questions

1. This passage is the last part of Martin Luther King Jr.'s speech, "I Have a Dream." Can you consider this to be a poem? If not, how is it different from other poems, for example, Walt Whitman's "I Hear America Singing"?

2. Martin Luther King Jr. uses many child images in his speech. What effects do these child images give to his speech? Who do you think the expression, "all of God's children," refer to?

Guide 5

What can you do with a poem? Write back to it!

Some readers believe that we read poetry in order to find "messages," which are valuable lessons that have been left for us by the writer. But what if the message is not valuable? What if it is in fact stupid or immoral? Or to say this in another way, what if the reader's view of the world is very different from the poet's view? Do we just have to give a "thumbs up" to the poets who have messages we like, and give a "thumbs down" to the poets whose messages we dislike?

No, there is another way. The reader can reply to the poet's work, respond with a different view of the world, or even compose a new poem. This kind of creative response—either an interpretation or a new poem—can help others see the original poem in new and interesting ways.

For instance, Walt Whitman wrote a famous poem called *Leaves of Grass* in which he again and again said he would reveal America's many voices: "I hear America singing, the varied carols I hear." But some readers might think that Whitman did not truly include authentic Black voices; his descriptions of Black Americans did not really let them speak for themselves. Perhaps that is one point of a poem by the famous Black poet Langston Hughes, who declares, "I, too, sing America. ... I, too, am America." By writing back to Whitman and responding to the gaps in Whitman's vision, Hughes offers us new, dynamic ways to see Whitman's poem, and new ways to perceive the realities of American culture. The more poems we read, the more wonderfully varied are the voices we can hear.

音声ファイルのダウンロード方法

英宝社ホームページ（http://www.eihosha.co.jp/）の
「テキスト音声ダウンロード」バナーをクリックすると、
音声ファイルダウンロードページにアクセスできます。

Understanding American Poetry
『アメリカ詩から学ぶアメリカ文化』

2019年1月15日　初　版　　　　　　2021年9月15日　第2刷

著　者 ©　　藤　野　功　一
　　　　　　C．S．ピ　ュ　ー
　　　　　　マット　セアド
　　　　　　高　橋　美知子

発　行　者　　佐　々　木　　元

発　行　所　株式会社　英　宝　社
〒101-0032 東京都千代田区岩本町2-7-7
Tel. [03] (5833) 5870　Fax. [03] (5833) 5872

ISBN978-4-269-07015-8 C1082
［組版：(株)マナ・コムレード / 印刷・製本：モリモト印刷 (株)］

本テキストの一部または全部を、コピー、スキャン、デジタル化等での
無断複写・複製は、著作権法上での例外を除き禁じられています。
本テキストを代行業者等の第三者に依頼してのスキャンやデジタル化は、
たとえ個人や家庭内での利用であっても著作権侵害となり、著作権法上
一切認められておりません。